HARVARD HISTORICAL MONOGRAPHS

XI

PUBLISHED UNDER THE DIRECTION OF THE DEPARTMENT
OF HISTORY FROM THE INCOME OF

THE ROBERT LOUIS STROOCK FUND

CHINESE TRADITIONAL HISTORIOGRAPHY

BY

CHARLES S. GARDNER

Cambridge
HARVARD UNIVERSITY PRESS
1961

DISTRIBUTED IN GREAT BRITAIN BY
OXFORD UNIVERSITY PRESS
LONDON

LIBRARY OF CONGRESS CATALOG CARD NUMBER 38-13532

PRINTED IN THE UNITED STATES OF AMERICA

TO MY FATHER

WHO HAS OPENED TO ME
THE LIFE OF SCHOLARSHIP

FOREWORD TO THE SECOND PRINTING

When Charles Sidney Gardner's *Chinese Traditional Historiography* first appeared in 1938, American and European scholars in Asian studies welcomed it with enthusiasm. For instance, "Dr. Gardner has rendered a real service to students of Sinology by this excellent little book," wrote the late Professor J. J. L. Duyvendak in the journal *T"oung pao;* Professor John K. Shryock's review in the *Journal of the American Oriental Society* expressed a similar evaluation.

Now, after some twenty-three years, this pioneer work is still found to contain much information and insight that students in the field cannot afford to overlook, and from which more advanced scholars continue to profit. This is evidenced in a recent publication of the Oxford University Press entitled *Historians of China and Japan*, edited by W. G. Beasley and E. G. Pulleyblank, containing articles by participants in a conference on Asian history held in London in 1956. A reading of the articles on China shows that several of the authors were building their contributions on the solid ground Gardner laid.

It seems certain that *Chinese Traditional Historiography* will continue to be required reading in the field for years to come. This second printing is brought out in response to undiminishing inquiries and requests, under the same sponsorship, that of the History Department of Harvard University, with the aid of a subsidy from the Harvard-Yenching Institute. Since Dr. Gardner's health does not permit him to do any extensive rewriting, the text is reproduced as first published, with a few pages of additions and corrections which I have prepared in consultation with him.

LIEN-SHENG YANG
Professor of Chinese History

Harvard University
July 1961

PREFACE

THE present small volume does not pretend to discover things new or strange. It rather aims at the systematic presentation of a part of those general ideas which are the necessary baggage of any historian who would handle the Chinese sources. It is intended primarily to smooth the path of the novice sinologist, to warn him of special perils and difficulties which beset his way, and to remind him of those canons of criticism which may help him to avoid some pitfalls. It is hoped that it may have some interest too for the professed historian in other fields who may have occasion to refer to Chinese sources in translation. It is with this latter reader in mind that an effort has been made to preserve the text as far as possible free from Chinese proper names and terminology, while still furnishing through footnotes to the specialist the indispensable minimum of concrete illustration and specific reference.

That this study has been prepared now, rather than a score of years hence, is due solely to the encouragement of my friend and colleague Professor Robert P. Blake. I am indebted to him also for calling to my notice the monumental and peculiarly stimulating work of Eduard Fueter, *Histoire de l'historiographie moderne* (Paris, 1914). Other friends, notably Professor L. C. Goodrich of Columbia and Professor J. J. L. Duyvendak of Leiden, have been kind enough to read and to point out some at least of the errors and inadequacies in the manuscript. My indebtedness is no less

deep to Edouard Chavannes (1865–1918), my unseen
master, whose example in bibliographic inquiry,
methodical analysis, critical appraisal and lucid exposition has been so brilliantly followed by Paul Pelliot
and Henri Maspero, like him of the Collège de France.
It is upon the work of these men, together with that of
Bernhard Karlgren, Rector of the University of Göteborg, that the present essay is largely based.

Because a large proportion of the numerous works
here cited, both books and periodical articles, contain
only scattered or incidental reference to the central
subject of this volume it has seemed rather futile to
gather them into a bibliography. It is hoped, however,
that the footnote references will suffice both for justification and for guidance.

The spelling of Chinese names and words in Roman
letters departs slightly from the more common usage
of Sir Thomas Wade's system, which was devised in
1859 for the use of Western students in China, and
modified by the late H. A. Giles in his *Chinese-English
Dictionary* (2nd edition, London, 1912). The present
further modification was first proposed by me in a
pamphlet, *A Modern System for the Romanization of
Chinese* (Cambridge, 1930), and was illustrated by a
syllabary in connection with my article, "The Western
Transcription of Chinese," published in the *Journal of
the North China Branch of the Royal Asiatic Society*
(LXII [1931], 137–147). Its objects are: (1) to enable
English speakers without special instruction to reproduce more nearly the Chinese sounds represented
originally by characters; (2) to eliminate some of the
most frequent causes of confusion between sounds,
resulting from errors in pronunciation or typography;

(3) to enlarge slightly the diversity of phonemes or distinctive sounds available for transcription, by recognition of certain historic distinctions of pronunciation which are still observed in large areas in China, but which have been lost in the Pekingese dialect alone represented by Wade and Giles.

The following brief table shows all of the modifications which are here made. The greater portion will be seen to flow from substitution of alternative initial letters of our alphabet for use of an arbitrary symbol, the inverted comma or apostrophe, as the sign of aspiration.

Wade: Initial p-, t-, k-, ts-	Modified: b-, d-, g-, dz-
" p'-, t'-, k'-, ts'-	p-, t-, k-, ts-
" ch-	j- and dz-
" ch'-	ch- " ts-
" hs-	hs- " s-
" j-	r-
Final -ih (ĭ)	-ir
" -ŭ, ŭ, -ᴢ'ŭ (ĭ)	-z

As a further aid to easy consultation, all Chinese proper names here cited will be found in the index under both their Giles-Wade and modified forms, with cross reference.

CHARLES S. GARDNER

Cambridge, Massachusetts
October 27, 1937

CONTENTS

PERIODICAL ABBREVIATIONS

BEFEO   *Bulletin de l'Ecole Française d'Extrême-Orient* (Hanoi).

BMFEA   *Bulletin of the Museum of Far Eastern Antiquities* (Stockholm).

GHÅ   *Göteborgs Högskolas Årsskrift* (Göteborg).

JA   *Journal Asiatique, Recueil trimestriel publié par la Société Asiatique* (Paris).

JNCBRAS   *Journal of the North China Branch of the Royal Asiatic Society* (Shanghai).

JRAS   *Journal of the Royal Asiatic Society of Great Britain and Ireland* (London).

MAO   *Mémoires concernant l'Asie Orientale, Académie des Inscriptions et Belles-Lettres* (Paris).

MCB   *Mélanges Chinois et Bouddhiques, Institut Belge des Hautes Etudes Chinoises* (Brussels).

TP   *T'oung Pao, Archives concernant l'Histoire, les Langues, la Géographie, l'Ethnographie et les Arts de l'Asie Orientale* (Leiden).

Three articles by Professor Bernhard Karlgren are here distinguished by conventional abbreviation:

Ancient Texts   "The Authenticity of Ancient Chinese Texts," BMFEA, I (1929), 165–183.

Early History   "The Early History of the *Chou li* and *Tso chuan* texts," BMFEA, III (1931), 1–59.

Tso chuan   "On the Authenticity and Nature of the *Tso chuan*," GHÅ, XXXII, no. 3 (1926), 1–65.

CHINESE TRADITIONAL
HISTORIOGRAPHY

CHAPTER I

Introduction: The New School of History

THE HISTORY of historical writing in China has not been written: it is a task far too vast to be undertaken here. An attempt will be made, however, to delineate in the following chapters those characteristics which distinguish sharply the traditional forms of Chinese history from most historical composition in Western lands.

Within the past two decades there has grown up in China a new school of history, new in inspiration, new in historical technique. This school seeks and finds one side of its ancestry among China's past historians. In fact, from dynasty to dynasty since the seventh century, a few bold, independent spirits have evolved the elements of historical (as distinguished from textual) criticism, despite the fact that their results were ignored or frowned upon by the orthodox.[1] During the seventeenth and eighteenth centuries especially, important advances were made towards the scientific method. Unfortunately, the forces of political and economic disintegration which had been unleashed during the closing decades of the Chien Lung era (1736–1795) so swiftly led to insurrection and other unmistakable signs of dynastic degeneracy, that all the energies of

[1] A. W. Hummel has clearly outlined both the succession of critical historians and the scholastic environment which largely nullified their efforts, in the introduction to his translation, *The Autobiography of a Chinese Historian* (顧頡剛 Gu Jieh-gang) (Leiden, 1931), pp. xviii–xxvii.

3

nineteenth-century scholars were absorbed in a vital
struggle for preservation of their inherited culture,
leaving them no leisure for its further re-evaluation and
criticism. The evolution of historical method was sus-
pended for a century.[2]

The renaissance of historical criticism and the introduction to China of modern scientific methodology are
acknowledged by present-day Chinese scholars as due
to the much maligned "impact of the West." [3] Enor-

[2] 崔述 Tsui Shu (1740–1816), last of the earlier line of critical
writers on method, died in obscurity without any successor. His
posthumous "Bequeathed Works," 崔東壁遺書 Tsui Dung-bi i
shu, 20 titles, 20 volumes, were reprinted in 1924 from a Japanese
edition. The 崔東壁年譜 ... nien pu, "Biography Year by
Year," by 姚紹華 Yao Shao-hua (Shanghai, 1931), contains a classified list of 35 titles by him.

[3] The first revival of historical criticism is traced by a recognized
leader of the new school, Gu Jieh-gang (1893–), to two books of
康有爲 Kang Yu-wei (1856–1927), who had "been much influ-
enced in his study of ancient Chinese history by the work done in
western lands." Hummel, Autobiography, p. 152. The books are
the 新學僞經考 Sin hsüeh wei jing kao, "Study of the Classics
Forged in the Sin Era" (A.D. 9–23), 14 chapters, 6 volumes (1891);
and the 孔子改制考 Kung Dz gai jir kao, "Study of Confucius
as a Reformer," 21 chapters, 6 volumes (1897). Although they
constitute an unscientific and unscrupulous attack (cf. infra, chap.
III, n. 19) upon the bulwarks of established political theory, these
books served in their time to demonstrate that even those venerable
literary monuments whose authenticity had been accorded biblical
immunity from question because of traditional connection with
Confucius might profitably be subjected to the ordeals of criticism.
    Gu acknowledges (Hummel, Autobiography, pp. 65–85, 152,
175) even greater indebtedness to the teaching of 胡適 Hu Shir
(1891–), who prepared his doctorate at Columbia in 1917, and who
has led, not only in creation of a new popular literature and in
revision of traditional ideas of the nation, but also in discovery of
Chinese precedents for Western scientific method. Three series of
胡適文存 Hu Shir wen tsun, "Literary Deposits," have been

mous influence has been and is being exerted, not only
by Western manuals of method [4] and by classic Western
models which are often neglected because written in
foreign languages, but even more by the personal teaching and example of Chinese scholars who have won
doctoral degrees from European and American uni-
versities.[5] The influence of these scholars might be

---

published by him, each in two 12mo western volumes (1921, 1924,
and 1930). The first has been reviewed by Paul Demiéville,
BEFEO, XXIII (1923), 489–499.

Both the political and the critical activities of 梁啓超 Liang
Chi-chao (1873–1929) were largely inspired by residence in the
United States. Both his 中國歷史研究法 Jung Guo li-shir
yen-jiu fa, "Methods of Research in Chinese History," which has
exhausted several editions since 1922, and to which a posthumous
"Supplement" (補編 bu bien) was issued in 1933, and his 要籍
解題及其讀法 Yao-dzi jieh-ti ji chi du-fa, "Criticism of Important Documents and Methods for Their Study," first issued in 1925,
have been largely influential.

Much of the activity of the new movement has been absorbed in
reappraisal of the texts and facts of antiquity. On these problems
252 essays, letters, and notes have been brought together in the
古史辨 Gu shir bien, "Symposium on Ancient History," 4 volumes (1926–1933). Three volumes are edited by Gu Jieh-gang,
who inserts his autobiography as introduction to the first; the
latest, which is devoted to philosophy, by 羅根澤 Lo Gen-dze.
A succinct conspectus of some of the more significant tentative
conclusions registered in the earlier stages of this discussion has
been presented by Hummel, "What the Chinese Are Doing in
Their Own History," American Historical Review, XXXIV (1928–
29), 715–724.

[4] Among those translated into Chinese may be noted C. V.
Langlois and Charles Seignobos, Introduction aux études historiques
(Shanghai, 1926); H. E. Barnes, The New History and the Social
Studies (Shanghai, 1933); and F. M. Fling, The Writing of History
(two translations, Beiping and Shanghai, 1933).

[5] The China Institute in America (New York) has compiled three
lists of Theses and Dissertations by Chinese Students in America,

even more fruitful had their teachers a more adequate conception of the radically foreign background which the students bring to their studies.[6] It is this purely Chinese background, and this alone, which forms the theme of the following pages.

---

presented for various degrees from 1902 to 1931. Of 1,162 theses, 336 are concerned with China.

[6] The Chinese students who come to this country are eager to secure the most rigorous training in method, but if not given explicit guidance in such matters as specific reference and systematic bibliography, they naturally tend to follow Chinese tradition, especially in their handling of Chinese sources.

CHAPTER II

Motivation

IT IS surely an axiom of all writing that the motives
which impel authorship largely condition the product.
Inasmuch as human nature is essentially the same the
world over, the historians of China and of the West
have been actuated by stimuli which are in the main
identical. It is, however, the comparatively rare points
of divergence which must here chiefly concern us.

The earliest Chinese historical texts derive from the
need to assist the memory in performance of sacri-
ficial rites due from the emperors or kings of the first
dynasties to their ancestors. Genealogical lists of sovereigns of the Hsia, Shang, and Jou dynasties, and of
various princely lines, form important constituents of
the "Annals Written on Bamboo," [1] of the classic

---

[1] 竹書紀年 *Ju shu ji nien,* an official chronicle of the state of
梁 Liang or 魏 Wei, ending in 299 B.C., and completed about the
same time by a chronicle of 晋 Dzin and of the whole empire since
high antiquity. Henri Maspero, *La Chine antique* (Paris, 1927),
p. xiii. The work was found in A.D. 281 in a tomb in the sub-prefecture of 汲 Ji near modern 衛輝府 Wei Huei Fu in Honan north
of the Yellow River. The tomb has been identified as that of King
襄 Siang or of a contemporary dignitary of Wei. The present name
of the work results from the fact that it was written, like all books
of its time, on slips of bamboo held together by thongs. Edouard
Chavannes, "Les livres chinois avant l'invention du papier," JA,
9e sér., V (1905), 5–75; M. A. Stein, "Notes on Ancient Chinese
Documents," *New China Review,* III (1921), 243–253. Chavannes
(*Les Mémoires historiques de Se-ma Ts'ien* [5 volumes, Paris, 1895–
1905], V, 446–479, esp. 447–461 and 464–468) translates the texts
which bear on discovery of the book and lists the chief sources for

"Canon of History," [2] and of sundry lesser compilations.[3] It is probable that throughout the primitive
period these genealogical records were a special care
of the diviners whose duty it was to inscribe the names

---

pre-Sung citations from it, which total approximately one-third of
the modern text. 王國維 Wang Guo-wei, who assembles these
fragments, 古本竹書紀年輯校, Part III in 海寧王忠慤公
遺書三集 his posthumously collected works, concludes from
evident discrepancies between them and the modern text that the
latter must be a forgery. Maspero, however, after closer analysis,
points out that the usual close agreement of the two versions suffices to authenticate the modern text as a whole, but that most of
the passages which do not appear or are altered in the modern editions are at variance with orthodox chronology. He concludes that
the text during the Sung period was unfortunately purged of these
variant passages, which, however, are proved by concordance of
external evidence to be exact in an important case in which the
accepted chronology is demonstrably mutilated. "La chronologie
des rois de Ts'i au IVe siècle avant notre ère," *TP*, XXV (1927–28),
367–386. Edouard Biot has translated the modern text, JA, 3e
sér., XII (1841), 537–578; XIII (1842), 381–431; as has also James
Legge, *The Chinese Classics*, vol. III, part I (Hongkong, 1865).

[2] 書經 *Shu jing* or 尚書 *Shang shu*, until the Han called simply
the *Shu*, a collection of documents concerning ancient China, composed between the ninth and sixth centuries B.C. Maspero, *La Chine
antique*, p. xii. Chavannes has pointed out that the relatively full
accounts presented by this work for the reigns of the heroic founders
and degenerate last representatives of each early dynasty represent
a later legendary accretion to the bare lists of genealogy. *Mémoires
historiques*, I, cxl–cxli. The "History" was included, like the
"Annals," among the works condemned to destruction by the First
Emperor of the Tsin dynasty in 213 B.C. This proscription was contemporaneous with a double revolution in the forms and materials
of writing, which resulted from substitution of more modern characters for the former archaic script and improvement of the hair
writing brush for use on roll silk, both of which accelerated the disappearance of early literature. During the period 179–157 B.C.,
29 chapters of the "History" were recovered in a fragmentary
manuscript by 伏生 Fu Sheng and transcribed by him in the 今文

of the royal progenitors, and the queries submitted for their decision, upon the sheep bones and tortoise shells which served as an oracle.[4]

jin wen, or new script. Some decades later, a manuscript in the 古文 *gu wen,* or ancient characters, having come to light, 孔安國 Kung An-guo professed to interpret from it 16 additional chapters; but this second reconstitution disappeared in the imperial archives. Between the years A.D. 317–322 梅賾 Mei Dze presented to the throne a *Shu jing* which included all 29 chapters of the "modern text," together with the lost additions, preface, and commentary of Kung An-guo, all of which latter were forged, perhaps by 王肅 Wang Su who died in 256, probably before discovery of the "Annals" in 281. Paul Pelliot, "Le Chou King en caractères anciens et le Chang chou che wen," MAO, II (Paris, 1916), 123–177, pl. XX–XXVI. This version is the one accepted as orthodox by the "old text" school of criticism and by Legge for his translation, *The Shoo King or the Book of Historical Documents,* 2 volumes (Hongkong, 1865). Only the half which reproduces the "modern text" of Fu Sheng can be used as authentic. Chavannes conveniently lists the chapters which originate with Fu, Kung, and the forger, *Mémoires historiques,* I, cxiii–cxxxvi.

[3] Among these the most important was the 世本 *Shir ben,* or "Genealogical Origins," which is said by 班彪 Ban Biao to have comprised in 15 chapters lists of emperors, kings, chief nobles, and high officials from the (fabulous) Yellow Emperor to the period 722–481 B.C. The lists were doubtless extended in later editions. Ban asserts that 司馬遷 Sz-ma Tsien used the work; but the latter does not mention it, explicitly citing instead the 帝繫姓 *Di hsi sing,* "Succession and Clans of the Emperors," or 五帝繫 *Wu di hsi,* "Succession of the Five Emperors," which may have been based upon the *Shir ben,* but which conforms to the late Jou theory of succession of five universal elements. The *Shir ben,* although lost, has been largely reconstituted from early citations by 張澍 Jang Ju in the 張氏叢書 *Jang Shir tsung shu,* "Collection of Mr. Jang." The *Di hsi sing* is preserved as section 63 in the 大戴禮記 *Da Dai li ji,* "Record of Rites of the Elder Dai." Chavannes, *Mémoires historiques,* I, cxli–cxliii.

[4] Such bones and shells which have been found since 1899 on the site of the last capital of the 商 Shang dynasty (? fifteenth–eleventh

With the growth of independence among the feudal
states into which the Jou kingdom gradually decom-
posed during the tenth to the eighth centuries B.C.,
separate archival records were prepared for each individual court. The chronicle of the state of 魯 Lu from
722 to 481 B.C. is preserved to us in somewhat condensed and garbled form under the name of "Spring
and Autumn Annals," [5] which was then a generic term
applied equally to the archival records of several other

---

centuries B.C. ?) largely corroborate the genealogy of its kings as
recorded in literary sources. W. P. Yetts, "The Shang-Yin Dynasty
and the An-yang Finds," JRAS (1933) pp. 657–685; and especially
H. G. Creel, *The Birth of China* (London, 1936). Flat bones or shells
were prepared for oracular purposes by boring conical holes from
the lower side very nearly to the surface, upon which was then
incised both the question for decision and the names of those immediate male ancestors to whom it was addressed. Upon local application of heat to the inscribed surface, diverging fissures appeared
(whence the pictographic character ト *bu*, "to divine"), and upon
these was based interpretation of the oracle. A single bone or shell
was used repeatedly until the surface was covered with writing and
the back closely pitted with holes. The recovered and transcribed
documents suffice to prove constant recourse to the oracle by the
late Shang kings, who seem to have ruled less by their own authority
than as representatives of their ancestral house. Many of the
inscriptions are signed by the diviners responsible for them. Ten
criteria for dating have been enunciated by 董作賓 Dung Dzo-bin,
甲骨文斷代研究例 *Jia-gu-wen duan-dai yen-jiu li*, "Rules for
Research in Dating Oracle Bone Inscriptions," in 慶祝蔡元培
先生六十五歲論文集 *Ching-ju Tsai Yüan-pei Sien-sheng liu-
shir-wu sui lun-wen dzi*, "Collection of Essays in Celebration of the
Sixty-fifth Year of Tsai Yüan-pei" (1933), I, 323–424.

[5] 春秋 *Chun tsiu*, literally "Springs and Autumns." Translation by Legge, *The Ch'un Ts'ew with the Tso Chuen* (*Chinese Classics*,
V), 2 volumes (Hongkong, 1872).

states.[6] Its preservation is owing chiefly to the fact
that it was edited by Confucius.[7]

The archival records of certain other states, 晋 Dzin,
楚 Chu, and 衛 Wei, were drawn upon about the close
of the fourth century B.C. by the unknown compiler of
a chronicle which was very soon afterward cut into
fragments and distributed as an addition to the small
ritual "Commentary of Dzo"[8] to the "Spring and

[6] The philosopher 墨翟 Mo Di of the fifth century B.C. speaks
(chap. XXXI) of the various *Chun tsiu* of 周 Jou, 燕 Yen, 宋 Sung,
and 齊 Tsi. Y. P. Mei, *The Ethical and Political Works of Motse*
(London, 1929), pp. 162–165.

[7] 孔丘 Kung Chiu, 551–479 B.C. or later? Inasmuch as his personal name is taboo from respect, he is called 孔子 Kung Dz, "the
philosopher Kung," or by his cognomen, 仲尼 Jung-ni, or by his
highest official title, 孔夫子 Kung Fu-dz, "the Hon. Kung."

[8] 左傳 *Dzo juan*. Legge's translation is cited *supra*, n. 5.
Bernhard Karlgren concludes from a careful linguistic analysis
("On the Authenticity and Nature of the Tso chuan," GHÅ,
XXXII, no. 3 [1926], 1–65), that the book has a distinctive and
homogeneous grammar of fourth century type, beyond the capacity
of a late forger. In a further study ("The Early History of the Chou
li and Tso chuan Texts," BMFEA, III [1931], 1–59, esp. 8–33, 42–
49, 53–55) he lists a long series of early citations amply sufficient to
establish the authentic early character of the work. Cf. *infra*,
chap. III, n. 31. With Ojima and Maspero he disproves Kang
Yu-wei's charges that the *Dzo juan* is a forgery of Liu Hsin. Cf.
infra, chap. III, no. 28. Maspero in his most recent study ("La
Composition et la date du Tso tchouan," MCB, I [1931–32], 137–
215), as in his *La Chine antique* (pp. 592–595), and in his review of
Karlgren's earlier article (JA, CCXII [1928], 159–165) stresses the
composite nature of the *Dzo juan*. The chronicle already mentioned
he defines ("La Composition," MCB, I, 191–193) as a general history of the struggle of the northern states, first 齊 Tsi and later
Dzin, against the southern state of Chu, from the middle of the
eighth century to the middle of the fifth, events being recorded with
reference to the chronology of Dzin. From facts mentioned directly
and indirectly in the text (cf. *infra*, chap. III, n. 22) it can hardly

Autumn Annals." This chronicle is now our most important source for the study of the feudal period. It may be presumed that the original archival records of these, as of the other states, excepting only victorious Tsin, were destroyed in the great proscription of 213 B.C., which aimed at suppression of precisely such local records because they constituted a moral barrier to unification of the empire. Those archives which may have escaped both the perils of war and deliberate destruction perished through the contemporary revolutions in the forms and materials of writing.

It has been remarked that the "Spring and Autumn Annals" are attributed to Confucius.[9] This scholar regarded himself, not as an historian, nor even pri-

have been compiled before the closing decades of the fourth century. A collection of astrological anecdotes contains erroneous references to the position of Jupiter calculated about the year 375 B.C. "La Composition," MCB, I, 172-173. Maspero traces also fragments of several early historical romances employed without criticism. *La Chine antique*, pp. 582-583, 585-587, 593-594. The terse ritual and ethical commentary upon the "Annals," which represents the distinctive teachings of an independent school analogous to those of the 公羊 *Gung Yang* and 穀梁 *Gu Liang* commentaries, contains erroneous mention of winter solstices and eclipses which must have been calculated between 352 and 238 B.C. "La Composition," MCB, I, 170-176, 188. Thus it appears that the major constituents of the text were composed about the same period, the close of the fourth century or shortly thereafter, and that their language was harmonized at the time of amalgamation. The composite work is already quoted by the third-century writers 荀子 Sün Dz and 韓非子 Han Fei Dz. *Ibid.*, pp. 190, 200-201.

[9] The great biography of Confucius inserted by Sz-ma Tsien among the annals of the princely houses in his "Historical Memoirs" (chap. XLVII), states very explicitly the fact of his authorship and cites the quotation by Mencius of the words of Confucius himself concerning it. Chavannes, *Mémoires historiques*, V, 283-435, esp. 420-423.

marily as a teacher, but rather as a statesman with a
practical if high-minded program of political conduct
— a program which, if adopted by the feudal princes
of his day, would put an end to the prevailing licen-
tiousness and violence. His object in editing the annals
of his native state of Lu was to exhibit by the lessons
of the past the rewards which are the infallible recom-
pense of the virtuous (as defined by his precepts) and
the calamities which overtake the vicious (those who
deviate from them). He sought to provide ideal precedents as a basis for sound moral judgments. Inasmuch
as the moral significance of the work outweighs its
incidental historical aspect, it is immaterial from the
compiler's viewpoint if the facts of history have been
altered or suppressed, the better to illustrate its dominant principles.[10]

The influence of the "Spring and Autumn Annals"
upon later history has been enormous. To it may be
traced the first authoritative expression of the idea
that political morality should be upheld by the historian, that it is a function and responsibility of his
calling to apportion praise and blame in due measure,
not by extended personal comment, but by the manner
and emphasis of his record. To trace in detail the modification and evolution of these ideas, which have played
a prominent role in the history of Chinese historiography, is quite beyond the scope of the present essay.
Suffice it to note that the union of political morality
with history received in the twelfth century A.D. the

---

[10] 吳康 Woo Kang presents an analysis of the work from this
standpoint in his *Les trois théories politiques du Tch'ouen Ts'ieou
interprétées par Tong Tchong-chou d'après les principes de l'école de
Kong-yang* (Paris, 1932), esp. pp. 172–181.

blessing of Ju Hsi,[11] a dynamic scholar whose authority
in later centuries may be compared to that of Aristotle
in medieval Europe, and whose digest of Chinese
history [12] remains today perhaps the most prominent
work of secondary historical reference.

Glorification is a motive which has actuated many
private as well as official historians, in China as in the
West. Some have been enjoined by imperial order [13]

[11] 朱熹 1131–1200. The biography of this genius is in the standard 宋史 Sung shir, "Sung History," chap. 429. H. A. Giles,
Biographical Dictionary, no. 446. More extended treatment, with
specific emphasis on philosophy, is given by J. P. Bruce, *Chu Hsi
and His Masters* (London, 1923).

[12] The 通鑑綱目 *Tung jien gang mu*, "Abridged View of the
'Comprehensive Mirror,'" 59 chapters, is introduced by a disquisition on the principles of history, dated 1172, by the master himself.
The body of the work, which covers the period 403 B.C.–A.D. 959, is
condensed under his direction from the much fuller and more objective 資治通鑑 *Dz jir tung jien*, "Comprehensive Mirror for Aid in
Government," 294 chapters, 80 volumes (Commercial Press reprint
of Sung edition, 1084), by 司馬光 Sz-ma Guang (1019–86). Both
works have been reprinted many times, provided with commentaries, and extended by supplements. Alexander Wylie, *Notes on
Chinese Literature* (Shanghai, 1867 and 1922), pp. 25–26; Robert des
Rotours, *Le Traité des examens* (Paris, 1932), pp. 74–82.

[13] It is only in altogether exceptional instances that any serious
effort has been made to control for the benefit of constituted authority the tenor of the historian's record. Imperial sponsorship of
historical composition, which has tended to be regarded as a dynastic obligation, does not traditionally carry with it any censorial
function. Most conspicuous exception is that of the Chien Lung
period, when a Manchu emperor attempted to expurgate from
Chinese literature all derogatory references to the Manchu people,
their Tungusic Jurjen predecessors, and their Mongol cousins.
L. C. Goodrich, *The Literary Inquisition of Ch'ien-lung* (Baltimore,
1935). The same emperor sponsored compilation of two histories
which were intended to place in a favorable, but misleading, light
the origins of his dynasty: the 皇清開國方略 *Huang-Tsing kai-
guo fang-lüeh*, "The Foundation of the Tsing Empire" (1773–89),

or stimulated by loyal sentiment (or the hope of imperial bounty) to record the glories of a dynasty or of an
emperor. Some have sought to render illustrious the
memory of a group, impelled by special ties of religion,[14]
loyalty to a school of learning,[15] community of scholarly
interest,[16] or local patriotism. Thanks to this last motive, China possesses by all odds the finest and most
complete series of local records in the world.[17] Finally,
it goes unsaid that innumerable documents owe their

---

translated by Erich Hauer (Berlin, 1926); and the 滿洲源流考
Man-jou yüan-liu kao, "Examination of the Origin of the Manchus"
(1777). He even ventured to revise, with the same intent, the
"Veritable Records" of his ancestors. Cf. *infra*, chap. VII, n. 15.

[14] Such is the inspiration for the work translated by Chavannes,
*Mémoire composé à l'époque de la grande dynastie T'ang sur les reli-
gieux éminents qui allèrent chercher la loi dans les pays d'occident,
par I-tsing* (Paris, 1894).

[15] Cf., e.g., the 清代樸學大師列傳 *Tsing dai pu hsüeh da shir
lieh juan*, "Biographies of the Great Masters of Unaffected Scholarship under the Tsing Dynasty," by 支偉成 Jir Wei-cheng, 2 western
volumes (Shanghai, 1924).

[16] Among such works may be cited the 疇人傳 *Chou ren juan*,
"Biographies of Mathematicians," by 阮元 Ruan Yüan, 46 chapters, 10 volumes (1799), with additions in subsequent editions. Cf.
notice of Louis van Hée, *Isis*, VIII (1926), 101–118.

[17] Not only is there an extensive gazetteer for each province,
containing *inter alia* its history, antiquities, and the biographies of
eminent native sons of all periods; but there is one of generally similar character for almost every prefecture, sub-prefecture, district,
and special area in the country. Many of these gazetteers have been
revised at frequent intervals; and for some areas there are two or
more entirely independent compilations. The National Library of
Beiping has published a special 方志書目 *Fang jir shu mu*, "Catalogue of Local Records," 4 volumes (1933), listing its unrivaled
collection of over 3,800 titles. The 中國地方志綜錄 *Jung-Guo
di-fang-jir dzung lu*, "Union List of Chinese Local Records," 3 volumes (1935), enumerates 5,832 editions held in China, Japan, and
the United States. Cf. *infra*, p. 102, n. 26.

genesis to friendship, loyalty, filial piety, or admiration for an individual.[18]

Three centuries and a half after the death of Confucius, a greater history than his was in process of compilation — a history which for the first time burst the bounds imposed by tradition. The private enterprise of two court astrologers, father and son, it became known to later ages as the "Historical Memoirs." [19] The leading motive of the elder historian, to judge by his final instructions to his son, was to win eternal fame by compilation of this work, for which he seems to have judged the time peculiarly propitious.[20] The son, 司馬遷 Sz-ma Tsien, has fortunately recorded his own motives.[21] History is to him no mere genealogical record, no bald archival chronicle of a single court, no

[18] Many biographies, especially for the Manchu period, have been reprinted in great repertories. A union index of 33 of these has been issued as no. 9 of the Harvard-Yenching Institute Sinological Index Series: 三十三種清代傳記綜合引得 San-shir-san-jung Tsing-dai juan-ji tsung-ho yin-de (Beiping, 1932). Numerous independent biographies in annal form, 年譜 nien pu, are appended to the collected works of single scholars.

[19] 史記 Shir ji, 130 chapters, 26 volumes (1739 edition). The translation by Chavannes of the first 47 chapters, Mémoires historiques, has already been repeatedly cited. Begun by 司馬談 Sz-ma Tan, who died in 110 B.C., the work was completed by his son, in part by 99, wholly before his death, which probably followed shortly that of the Emperor Wu in 87 B.C. Mémoires historiques, I, xxi–xxii, xliv–xlv. Sz-ma himself refers to his work as 太史公書序 Tai Shir Gung shu sü, "The History and Preface of His Honor, the Grand Astrologer," a title which with various slight abridgments was employed throughout the Han period. Woo Kang, Les trois théories politiques, p. 176, n. 3.

[20] Chavannes, Mémoires historiques, I, xxii–xxiii.

[21] In the final chapter (CXXX) of his work, which is devoted to the biographies of his father and himself. Chavannes, Mémoires historiques, I, vii–lxi, esp. lviii–lix.

treatise on political morality. Nor is it dedicated to the glory of any individual or institution. Rather it is a composite portrayal of the whole past of his whole people, so far as accessible documents permit such a record. Especially is it a golden opportunity for the judicious historian to render justice to the worthy, and by the fullness of his narrative to rescue them from threatened oblivion, even as he unflinchingly records the depths of human degradation.[22] It is surely no reflection upon his moral stature if he becomes as fully aware as was his father that, by realization of his aim objectively to record the glory and depravity of others, he at the same time makes secure his own immortality.

Objective detachment is, to be sure, already exemplified by the great feudal chronicle in the "Commentary of Dzo." Sz-ma Tsien, in adhering to this tradition, by the great weight of his influence did much to establish it as an obligation for later writers of history. In fact, despite the profound veneration accorded to the personal work of Confucius, and elaboration of his ideas by Ju Hsi, objective scholarship has proved the commonest as well as the highest inspiration to Chinese historians. Indeed, as will be seen in more detail in a later chapter, an assumption of complete objectivity underlies the whole Chinese conception of historical writing.

[22] Doubtless also, in his account of his own times, he gives expression to a natural desire to satirize an over-superstitious court, which as astrologer he knew too well. Chavannes, *Mémoires historiques*, I, lii–liii.

CHAPTER III

TEXTUAL CRITICISM

IT SHOULD be said at the outset that the Chinese are not a whit behind Western scholarship in the exacting domain of textual or preparatory criticism, that discipline which is concerned with the authentication, establishment, and meaning [1] of texts, but not with their historical appraisal and utilization. Imperial proscription in 213 B.C. of most early historical and philosophical literature, which had been cited with embarrassing effect by opponents of needed reform, led inevitably to vigorous efforts at recovery when the ban was finally lifted.[2] In fact, it may be claimed without exaggeration that textual criticism has absorbed much of the attention of the best Chinese scholars from the second century before Christ to our own day.

Certainly the canons of criticism were not developed by one man, nor by a single generation. Indeed, they have never received any purely Chinese systematization and logical expression such as western theory has

---

[1] Meaning is certainly a concern of historical criticism but is no less essential to intelligent conjectural emendation.

[2] All the odium of this proscription has been heaped upon its author, 李斯 Li Sz, and the First Emperor of the Tsin who put it into effect; but it was found so helpful to the new unification of North China (the civilized known world) that it was continued by the first emperors of the Han, despite a fruitless appeal by 陸賈 Lu Jia in 196, until finally revoked in 191 B.C. Edouard Biot, *Essai sur l'histoire de l'instruction publique en Chine et de la corporation des lettrés* (Paris, 1847), pp. 95-96.

enjoyed.[3] Rather they have been evolved, applied, and transmitted through the inspiration of concrete example. As a consequence, while the most brilliant results have been achieved by many scholars, application of critical principles has been, among others, both partial and uncertain.[4]

A century before Christ the critical judgment of Sz-ma Tsien, whose "Historical Memoirs" were to provide the model for the standard histories of later dynasties, as in all former times was still expressed chiefly by the primitive device of inclusion or exclusion of available material.[5] Although Sz-ma permitted himself the liberty of adding personal remarks at the

---

[3] It is in part the consciously systematic application of identical principles which has enabled the sinological Titans of the Collège de France — Chavannes, Pelliot, and Maspero — to advance their research upon the foundation of, but beyond, the results obtained by native Chinese scholarship.

[4] Karlgren has sought to identify and illustrate ten of the principles of Chinese criticism, with the particular object of helping Chinese historians to avoid past weaknesses: "The Authenticity of Ancient Chinese Texts," BMFEA, I (1929), 165–183. Cf. the notice by Pelliot, TP, XXVII (1930), 221, and especially the review by Maspero, JA, CCXXII (1933), "Bulletin critique," pp. 38–48. Karlgren has published two other articles on textual criticism: "On the Authenticity and Nature of the Tso chuan," GHÅ, XXXII (1926), no. 3, reviewed by Maspero, JA, CCXII (1928), 159–165; and "The Early History of the Chou li and Tso chuan Texts," BMFEA, III (1931), 1–59. These three articles by Karlgren will hereafter be distinguished as Ancient Texts, Tso chuan, and Early History, respectively.

[5] Thus, as Chavannes has pointed out, he reproduces much of the "modern text" of the "Canon of History," but ignores all but one of the further chapters which purported to be based on an "ancient text," and which must have been known to him. *Mémoires historiques*, I, cxiii–cxxxvi. For a summary account of the texts of the *Shu jing*, cf. *supra*, chap. II, n. 2.

close of each formal chapter, these are very brief and perforce general in character. Down until the close of the Former Han period (or about the beginning of the Christian era) those extensive commentaries which had clustered about the classic texts were transmitted as separate works.[6]

Expression of criticism, both textual and factual, has been greatly favored by adoption of a simple device, comparable to the Western footnote, for differentiation of comment from the text to which it relates. In its simplest and presumably earliest form this consists in merely reducing the size of characters for the commentary, which is accordingly recognized as such, and may be distributed through the text, phrase by phrase if that be desired.[7]

An obvious defect in the scheme lies in the danger that a careless copyist may ignore the intended distinction of size and transcribe the comment as part of the text.[8] That danger is largely avoided by an improve-

---

[6] Karlgren has called attention to a preface in which 段玉裁 Duan Yü-tsai (1735–1815) stresses this point, 皇清經解 *Huang Tsing jing jieh*, "Classical Comment of the Tsing Dynasty," chap. 600, 1a.

[7] Among the Buddhist manuscripts rescued by Pelliot from the tenth-century cache at Dun Huang (cf. *infra*, p. 45) is one arranged in this manner. Pelliot, "Une bibliothèque médiévale retrouvée au Kan-sou," BEFEO, VIII (1908), 509–510. Possibly the 前漢書藝文志 *Tsien Han shu, I wen jir*, "Essay on Literature" in the standard "History of the Former Han" (cf. *infra*, p. 35), is among the earliest works to employ this expedient: the brief comments of the compiler, 班固 Ban Gu (A.D. 32–92), are appended directly to the items of this bibliography.

[8] As 全祖望 Tsüan Dzu-wang (1705–55) brilliantly points out, such seems to have been in fact the fate of the subcommentary within the 水經注 *Shui jing ju*, "Commentary on the 'Water Clas-

ment introduced by Ma Rung [9] in the second century.
The smaller characters of the commentary are arranged
in a double column within the space normally occupied
by a single column of text. Thus, not only are the
reader and copyist warned by contrast in size and
arrangement, but double the volume of comment can
be inserted without enlarging the page. Indeed, Sz-ma
Tsien's own work, in the latest official edition (1739)
of the standard histories, is accompanied by three
elaborate commentaries, distributed *pari passu* through
the text, and distinguished one from another by short
titles which are printed as black backgrounds framing
white characters.

Most Chinese historical works, as will be seen more
in detail in a following chapter, embody numerous
direct verbal loans from earlier literature. It follows
as a necessary consequence that the study of filiation
of texts assumes particular importance and presents
problems of peculiar delicacy. Filiation is established
precisely as in Western practice, in absence of or supplement to other criteria, by comparison of borrowed or
parallel passages.

Evidently a loan may be made in either of two ways:
the original text may be reproduced inviolate with

sic,'" composed at the beginning of the sixth century. Pelliot,
BEFEO, VIII, 509–510; 鄭德坤 Jeng De-kun, 水經注引得 ...
yin de, "Index to the 'Water Classic and Commentary'" (Harvard-
Yenching Institute Sinological Index Series, no. 17), 2 volumes
(Beiping, 1934), I, xiv–xv.

    [9] 馬融 (79–166), biography in 後漢書 *Hou Han shu*, the
standard "History of the Later Han," XCa; Giles, *Biographical
Dictionary*, no. 1475. Maspero asserts that the innovation first
appears in Ma's commented edition of the 周禮 *Jou li*, "Jou
Ritual," A.D. 138–140. "La Composition," MCB, I (1931–32), 183.

identical phraseology, or the wording may be altered while the sense is preserved. In the former case, one of the passages with identical wording is apt to reveal itself as a loan by contrast of language, style, spirit, or ideas with the text in which it has been inserted. It is even quite possible to observe identical passages both or all of which are plainly loans from an unidentified original. In the event that the secondary character of neither passage can be detected with sufficient assurance to establish priority, there remains no course but to register existence of the parallel. Even in such a case, a probability of the direction of the loan may appear from the character of the works in question: one may be a largely original work of established authenticity; the other, a comparatively obscure text containing identical or close parallels with several well-known works,[10] and already subject to suspicion of forgery because of gaps in its record of transmission. When, in the process of borrowing, phraseology has been altered, it is usually possible by confrontation of the various versions to establish filiation. Evidently, if the alterations be slight, the difficulty is proportionally enhanced and may even be insurmountable; [11]

[10] Karlgren (Ancient Texts, BMFEA, I, 171–172) considers this point, but dismisses it because it fails to yield final proof. As elsewhere in this article, he ignores the fact that history is concerned far more often with probabilities than with facts which are susceptible of scientific demonstration.

[11] Karlgren (Ancient Texts, BMFEA, I, 171) proposes to distinguish cases of slight alteration as a category altogether separate from paraphrase, and even dogmatically asserts the former to be "absolutely valueless" for authenticity argumentation, whereas the latter makes filiation "easy to determine." Such arbitrary division is inadmissible in theory and threatens to be ridiculous in practice,

but, again, a probability may sometimes be ascertained even when certainty is unattainable.

In approaching the question of authorship, a distinction must be drawn between Chinese and Western ideas of authenticity. Few writers of the pre-Han epoch (prior to the second century B.C.) are really known to us. Even when a name has been preserved, this is an illusory label, which fails to inform us seriously concerning the personality and motives of the author or of his qualifications for authorship. It is then almost a matter of indifference whether we do or do not attach a personal name to an early text. The principle just enunciated, which is become a commonplace of Western historical thinking, has not yet received recognition at the hands of all Chinese scholars. Much has been and is being written in China to disprove alleged connection of individual names with specific texts. And some critics have lost sight of the intrinsic importance of early documents simply because previous allegations concerning their authorship have proved unfounded.[12]

since there is no logical standard or boundary by which to determine to which class any border-line case belongs. Maspero (review of Ancient Texts, JA, CCXXII [1933], "Bulletin Critique," pp. 44–45) has shown with an instructive example invoked by Karlgren himself (BMFEA, I, 174–175), that the latter is mistaken in a particularly delicate determination of filiation between three variant but closely parallel texts. To which category does this case belong?

[12] Karlgren's illustration of this, his fifth criterion (Ancient Texts, BMFEA, I, 167), is not particularly happy. He notes that 晁公武 Chao Gung-wu (died 1171, cf. Pelliot, "Le Chou King en caractères anciens," MAO, II, 152, n. 1; also BEFEO, XIII [no. 7], 46) has shown statements concerning the author of the early text known by the empty name 尹文子 Yin Wen Dz, "Philosopher Yin Wen," are not correct; and that 宋濂 Sung Lien (1310–81) has adduced evidence proving that the preface which contains these

Paradoxically enough, in the case of modern texts, when no doubt of authenticity exists, the Chinese have shown considerable complaisance towards nominal indications of authorship. The names of sponsors of publication are sometimes substituted for those of the actual authors or compilers.[13]

statements is itself a forgery. Karlgren concludes, perhaps a trifle hastily, that Sung's further imputation that the text is also spurious is based merely on association with the fraudulent preface. The remarks of Chao and Sung are reproduced with tacit approval by 姚際恆 Yao Dzi-heng (1647–1715?) in his 古今僞書考 Gu jin wei shu kao, "Investigation of Forgeries of Ancient and Modern Times," edition punctuated by Gu Jieh-gang (1929), pp. 30–31. It appears likely that Chao, Sung, and Yao had serious grounds for distrust of the current text, even though they did not specifically adduce them. 唐鉞 Tang Yüeh, in the course of a long examination of the work in the 清華學報 Tsing Hua Journal, IV, no. 1 (June 1927), 1153–74, has shown abundant cause for impeaching its authenticity. Part of this study is reproduced in the Gu jin wei shu kao bu jeng 補證, "tested and augmented" version of Yao's book, compiled by 黃雲眉 Huang Yün-mei (Nanking, 1932), pp. 137–142.

[13] The well-known 書目答問 Shu mu da wen, "Answers to Queries on Bibliography," was published in 1875 in the name of 張之洞 Jang Jir-dung. That it was actually compiled by his then secretary 繆荃孫 Miao Tsüan-sun is generally accepted in Chinese bibliographic circles. Cf., e.g., the Shu mu da wen bu jeng 補正, the "augmented and corrected" edition of the original work, by 范希曾 Fan Hsi-dzeng, 2 volumes (Nanking, 1931), preface, 1b2. None the less, it regularly is listed as the work of Jang—even in the 三訂國學用書撰要 San ding guo hsüeh yung shu juan yao, "Thrice Edited Selection of Books Important for Sinological Study," by 李笠 Li Li (Peking, 1927), prelim. pp. 1, 3, text 76. Karlgren (Ancient Texts, BMFEA, I, 169) follows this practice, which is the more remarkable in that Miao subsequently earned a great reputation as bibliographer, librarian, editor, and archaeologist. BEFEO, VI, 403, n. 1; IX, 829, n. 1; XII (no. 9), 63, 65, 89. Similarly, the famous 皕宋樓藏書志 Bi Sung Lou tsang shu jir, the catalogue published in 1882 of rarities in the library of 陸心源 Lu

Maspero has pointed out [14] the preponderant importance of anachronism as a criterion in the Chinese
processes of internal textual criticism. Discovery of
one anachronism serves to invalidate at least the particular portion of the text in which it is found, and may,
with other instances, suffice to disprove utterly authenticity of the whole.[15] It is nevertheless essential to bear
constantly in mind the relatively great frequency of
interpolation in the transmission of Chinese texts:
interpolation or at least intercalation, particularly in
case of anachronism, is always to be suspected.

Interpolation most often results from editorial activity and may spring from various motives. An editor
may wish to continue an historical account by insertion
of later relevant facts, or to enrich it with additional
material of interest.[16] He may seek to correct supposed

Sin-yüan, which is uniformly attributed to that scholar, appears
to be the work of 李宗蓮 Li Dzung-lien who contributes a preface
to it. Pelliot summarizes a study of the library by 島田彥楨
Shimada Gentei to whom the original manuscript of the catalogue
was presented, BEFEO, IX (1909), 466, n. 3.

[14] In his masterly review of Karlgren's article, Ancient Texts,
already cited (cf. *supra*, this chap., n. 4).

[15] Karlgren's criterion no. 1, Ancient Texts, BMFEA, I, 166. By
way of illustration he cites the demonstration by 陳振孫 Chen
Jen-sun (thirteenth century) that the study of references to natural
history in Mao's version of the "Odes," 毛詩草木鳥獸蟲魚疏
Mao Shir tsao mu niao shou chung yü su, must be later than the
commentary of 郭璞 Guo Po (276–324) from which it quotes. It
is then rather disconcerting when, in a later article (Early History,
BMFEA, III, 12) he still cites this work as "of 陸璣 Lu Ki (third
century A.D.)" without any qualification.

[16] Such is the origin of a whole series of interpolations in Sz-ma's
"Historical Memoirs," by 褚少孫 Chu Shao-sun who, no doubt
proudly, affixed his name to most of them. Chavannes, *Mémoires
historiques*, I, cciv–ccix.

inaccuracies,[17] or even to alter the entire framework of dating to conform to ideas of chronology which are current in his own time.[18] He may desire to restore the text to completeness by insertion of passages found elsewhere and which he believes once belonged to it. He may aim to harmonize the text with other documents. All of these motives are plainly innocent in intention. On the other hand, he may desire to "find" (insert) in an unquestionably genuine early text authentication or justification for forged documents or later ideas, his own or those of someone whose good will he covets.[19] Finally, intercalation may result simply from

[17] Such was presumably the motive of the editor who, according to the convincing hypothesis of Maspero (review of Ancient Texts, JA, CCXXII, 43–44), "corrected" the original reading of the "Essay on Literature" in the *Han shu*, which presumably assigned 18 sections to the ancient 管子 *Guan Dz*, by substituting the number 86, that of the current forgery of the same name.

[18] It has been already noted (*supra*, chap. II, n. 1) that the chronology of the whole "Annals Written on Bamboo" was falsified in this way during the Sung period, to bring it into conformity with the then orthodox system which was calculated by 劉歆 Liu Hsin, sponsored by Ban Gu (cf. *infra*, this chap., n. 38), and stamped with the seal of approval by 司馬光 Sz-ma Guang (1019–86), who adopted it for his great "Comprehensive Mirror for Aid in Government" (cf. *supra*, chap. II, n. 12). Léopold de Saussure has exposed the illusory bases of this system in his article, "Sur l'inanité de la chronologie chinoise officielle," JA, CCIII (1923), 360–362.

[19] To the honor of Chinese scholarship be it said that such interpolations are conspicuously rare. A false impression of their prevalence can be traced to the sweeping but libelous charges which were publicized by 康有爲 Kang Yu-wei, the politician who in 1898 attempted a radical and too rapid reform of the imperial government, resulting in his own flight and the incarceration of the emperor by the empress-dowager. Cf. *supra*, chap. I, n. 3. M. E. Cameron, *The Reform Movement in China, 1898–1912* (Stanford, 1931). Kang alleged, with the motive of weakening the conservative political authority of the classics, that wholesale interpolation and forgery,

a scribal error, the incorporation into a text of what was originally an annotator's gloss or comment.[20]

Anachronism may take various forms. One of these is citation within a document of a later (or spurious) text.[21] Evidently in such a case it is essential to establish priority of filiation — that it is not the later compiler or forger who did the borrowing. Anachronism in data may be clearly perceptible through open statement of events or facts of a later period, or may be concealed in the form of prophecy which implies afterknowledge.[22] Ideas, too, have their own history and

notably of the *Dzo juan* and *Jou li*, were practiced in the opening years of the Christian Era by Liu Hsin, with the object of supporting the innovations of his patron, the usurper 王莽 Wang Mang. Evidence amply sufficient to expose the groundlessness of this defamatory claim, in so far as the *Dzo juan* and *Jou li* are concerned, has been adduced by Ojima, Karlgren, and Maspero. Cf. *infra*, this chap., n. 28; n. 31; and chap. IV, n. 6.

[20] The striking instance of the "Water Classic and Commentary" has already been cited, *supra*, chap. III, n. 8.

[21] Karlgren (Ancient Texts, BMFEA, I, 170) considers citation of a spurious text as a separate criterion (no. 8). Closer examination shows, however, that the feature of a spurious text which is important in this connection is not its character as such, but its posterior period of production. A later writer may in good faith cite an earlier forgery without thereby himself incurring suspicion. Very numerous reputable authors have mistakenly accepted and drawn upon the "ancient text" of the "Canon of History."

[22] Maspero in his review of Karlgren's Tso chuan (JA, CCXII [1928], 162–163), and more in detail in his "La Composition" (MCB, I, 191–192), points out that the chronicle within the *Dzo juan* contains three early "predictions" of late events: under date of 661 B.C., elevation of the lords of 魏 Wei to princely rank, secured in 403; under 629, transfer of the 衛 Wei capital three centuries later (actually 330–320); and under 606, loss of the imperial Jou tripods seven centuries after 1027, concording perfectly with the historic date 327 B.C.; all of which tend to prove that the work was compiled after this latest date.

may betray a posterior epoch of composition. The evolution of the Chinese language and script has in every period of history added new verbal expressions and new forms and usages of characters.[23] Grammatical evolution has been perhaps less constant, but still serves as a useful criterion in the case of early texts. Homogeneity of linguistic structure of an early type, beyond the capacity of any later forger, is in itself an adequate proof of authenticity.[24] Style, too, affords a criterion to the discerning critic. Unfortunately, style is peculiarly difficult to analyze, and doubtless many judgments have been hazarded on this ground with inadequate foundation.[25] Still, it is surely true that a stylistic argument which is advanced by an erudite and cautious Chinese critic who has spent much of his

[23] Particularly useful in the search for anachronism are posthumous titles and temple names unguardedly employed "before" their conferment; and incomplete, distorted, or substitute characters employed to avoid others which have become temporarily taboo (cf. *infra*, pp. 82–84).

[24] Karlgren has provided a new tool for the study of early documents by analysis of grammatical particles in the language of the *Dzo ₒjuan*, and its comparison with other early texts. Tso chuan, GHA, XXXII, 30–65. Reverting to the matter in his later study (Ancient Texts, BMFEA, I, 176–183, criterion no. 10), he suggests that this criterion is valid only if local dialects are in question, not if, as Maspero has supposed (review, JA, CCXII [1928], 164–165), the grammatical homogeneity springs from stylistic normalization of an editor. We may agree with Karlgren that "style is . . . an artificial phenomenon, the essence of which is imitation." But it remains true that no later writer has ever successfully imitated the style of the *Dzo juan*.

[25] Karlgren (Ancient Texts, BMFEA, I, 167, criterion no. 4) demands that "one has to show which peculiarities of style are decisive," failing which, personal judgments "should be totally disregarded."

life and best powers in observation and creation of
literary style must carry serious weight, even though
he be unable to analyze the grounds for his decision.[26]

Chinese critics have sometimes impugned the genu-
ineness of a text on the ground, closely allied to anachronism, that its character is "shallow and vulgar."
No doubt again this basis of judgment has been often
abused.[27] Are all Western critics above censure? It
must still be allowed that no document of any kind
which contains only shallow ideas badly expressed has
any chance of achieving fame among a community of
scholars, much less of receiving the ultimate accolade
of painstaking transmission through many centuries.
A shallow and vulgar text which claims descent from
the pre-Han epoch has every chance of being a forgery.
In this case, as in that of style, an essential element in
the matter is to be sought in the personal qualification
of the critic.

To consider finally one criterion of constructive
internal criticism, presence in the current text of citations from other documents which, by reason of con-

[26] Pelliot has noted that in such matters the Chinese are better
judges than we. "Autour d'une traduction sanscrite du Tao To
King," TP, XIII (1912), 367.

[27] Karlgren (Ancient Texts, BMFEA, I, 166–167, 183, criterion
no. 3) characterizes it as "curious and naive," and again takes the
extreme position, "it is high time that this criterion was definitely
eliminated from the discussions on authenticity." He cites con-
flicting judgments on 鶡冠子, "Philosopher Ho Guan," passed
by two Tang essayists, 韓愈 Han Yü and 柳宗元 Liu Dzung-
yüan. These two, however, are not primarily textual critics,
and their judgment on such a work as Ho Guan Dz might fairly
be expected to differ, in view of their famous altercation over
Buddhism.

tent or form must have been repugnant to a possible forger, offers strong positive evidence of authenticity.[28]

External control of ancient documents is often possible through contemporary or early citations from them [29] in other texts of known reliability. Authentication is feasible if the present text can be shown to be in identical agreement with such citations which were necessarily unknown to a possible forger, which were so numerous as to preclude his use of all of them,[30] or

[28] Karlgren (Early History, BMFEA, III, 42–44) cites 29 quotations from the "Odes" in the *Dzo juan*, and shows that these differ from Mao's version of them which 劉歆 Liu Hsin strongly favored. He draws the plain conclusion that Liu can have neither forged nor freely altered the *Dzo juan*. The same evidence had already been advanced by 小島 Ojima, "On the texts of the Confucian canons quoted in the Tso chuan," 支那學 *Shinagaku*, III (1923), 50–61, 127–139, 452–468, esp. 50–60, as noted by Maspero in his elaborate refutation of the charges that the *Dzo juan* was falsified by Liu, "La Composition," MCB, I, 137–215, esp. 143, n. 2. Maspero, *ibid.*, 177–178, draws attention to an even more striking instance of the same kind. The "Spring and Autumn Annals" record an eclipse of the 27th year of Duke 襄 Siang (546 B.C.) in the 12th month. We know that Liu Hsin himself calculated that this eclipse belonged in the 9th month, for his astronomical results are reported in the "History of the Former Han," XXVII, 五行志 *Wu hsing jir*, "Essay on the Five Influences," sec. V, 9a9–10, 9b10, and *passim*. Yet, instead of "correcting" the *Dzo juan* to agree with the "Annals" or with his own computation, he preserved its anomalous independent reading "11th month," together with a cyclical indication which belonged properly to the 9th month.

[29] Mention alone suffices to establish only the early existence of a work of similar name, not the authenticity of the text now current under that name.

[30] The text of the "Annals Written on Bamboo" is controlled through citation by at least thirteen pre-Sung authors, one of whom alone refers to it over one hundred times. By this means, as already noted (*supra*, chap. II, n. 1), Maspero is able not only to declare the modern text basically sound, but to indicate the process of chronological emendation to which it was subjected in Sung times.

which were plainly prejudicial to his known interests.
It is also possible if it can be shown that the authenti-
cated citations stand in secondary relation to the present
text.[31] Absence from a modern text of passages which
may have been preserved elsewhere by early citation
is no cause for concern if it can be shown that a portion
or portions of the original work have been lost in transmission. On the other hand, discovery among early
citations of passages which are present in strongly
variant or altogether distorted form in the modern text,
or of extensive passages which are entirely lacking from
a current text that purports to be complete, constitutes
strong evidence of forgery.[32]

[31] Thus Karlgren (Early History, BMFEA, III, 35–41) demon-
strates by 28 examples of loans from each that the 周禮 *Jou li* and
Dzo juan texts were known to 毛亨 Mao Heng and 毛萇 Mao
Chang, the father and son who were responsible for the 毛傳 *Mao
juan* or "Mao Commentary on the 'Odes,'" prior to the middle of the
second century B.C. (*ibid.*, pp. 12–33). He cites (*ibid.*, pp. 50–52)
14 glosses of the *Jou li* and 10 of the *Dzo juan* in the 爾雅 *Er ya*, a
classified glossary of the third or early second century B.C. (*ibid.*,
pp. 44–49, 53–54); together with (*ibid.*, p. 55) a list of 31 references
to the *Dzo juan* previously identified by Chavannes in Sz-ma's
"Historical Memoirs" of about 100 B.C. Already in his earlier
article, Tso chuan (GHÅ, XXXII, 24–49), Karlgren had cited
23 of these parallel passages, pointing out Sz-ma's secondary paraphrase of difficult expressions.

[32] 江聲 Jiang Sheng (1721–1799) has reconstructed from ancient
citations most of the 大誓 *Tai shir* or "Grand Harangue," a chapter of the "Canon of History" which was recovered in the first
century B.C. from a text in archaic script, and subsequently lost.
皇清經解 *Huang Tsing jing jieh*, chap. 394, 1a–11b. This text is
reproduced and translated by James Legge, *Chinese Classics*, vol. III,
part 2, pp. 298–299. He notes a somewhat variant but basically
similar reconstruction by 王鳴盛 Wang Ming-sheng in the same
collection, chap. 413. Contrast of these authentic fragments with
the version of the "same" chapter which was presented to the

The Chinese, perhaps better than any other people, are able to control the history of transmission of their early texts, thanks primarily to their possession of an unparalleled series of bibliographic records.

It will be recalled that the proscription of literature in 213 B.C. was followed by a determined effort at recovery during the succeeding centuries. That reaction proceeded with cumulative effect and was greatly intensified by appointment in 136 B.C. of an imperial commission for recovery of the classics, and by establishment in 124 B.C. of a national college for the classical training of civil officials.[33] Compilation of the first imperial inventory of literature is most authoritatively recorded by 班固 Ban Gu [34] in his standard "History of the Former Han Dynasty." [35]

---

throne by Mei Dze in 317–322 proves the latter to be a complete forgery. Karlgren, Ancient Texts, BMFEA, I, 166, criterion no. 2; Chavannes, *Mémoires historiques*, I, cxxviii; cf. *supra*, chap. II, n. 2.

[33] Biot, *Essai sur l'histoire de l'instruction publique*, pp. 101, 103–118. Foundation of the college was a tardy realization of the proposal of 董仲舒 Dung Jung-shu in 140 B.C. Maspero has pointed out that all the cultural activity of the second century under imperial auspices is properly traceable to the unremitting pressure of the scholar class. "La Composition," MCB, I, 194–197.

[34] A.D. 32–92. N. L. Swann, *Pan Chao: Foremost Woman Scholar of China* (New York, 1932), pp. 27–28, 62–73; 鄭鶴聲 Jeng Ho-sheng, 班固年譜 *Ban Gu nien pu* (Shanghai, 1931); Lo Tchen-ying, *Une famille d'historiens et son oeuvre* (Études et documents, Institut Franco-Chinois de Lyon, vol. IX, Paris, 1931). Miss Lo places Ban Gu's death in A.D. 91.

[35] 前漢書藝文志 *Tsien Han shu, I wen jir*, the "Essay on Literature," often elliptically cited as the *Han jir*, preface, XXX, 1b4–2a3. The whole passage has been translated by James Legge, *Chinese Classics*, I, 3–4; but the present version adheres to the original more closely than his. The rendering of titles of Han functionaries follows the 辭源 *Tz yüan*, "Encyclopedic Dictionary"

By the reign of the Emperor Cheng (成帝, 32–7 B.C.), as books were becoming scattered and lost, he employed Reception Chamberlain Chen Nung to seek surviving works throughout the empire. He decreed that Court Consultant 劉向 Liu Hsiang should collate the classics and their commentaries, the works of all schools of philosophy, poetry and rhymed prose; that Infantry Guard Officer Ren Hung should collate books on war; Grand Astrologer Yin Hsien those on the natural and occult sciences; and Physician-in-Waiting Li Ju-guo those on drugs. As each work was finished [Liu] Hsiang immediately itemized its table of sections [36] and prepared an abstract of its contents. These were recorded and presented to the emperor. Meantime Hsiang died, but the Emperor Ai [哀帝, 6–2 B.C.] further employed Hsiang's son, the Imperial Equerry [Liu] 歆 Hsin, to complete his father's work. Hsin thereupon grouped all the books and presented to the throne his "Seven Summaries." Thus we have: the "General Summary," the "Summary of the Six Classics," and those of "All Philosophers," "Poetry and Rhymed Prose," "Military Literature," "Divination," and "Pharmacology." Now we edit their essentials to provide a bibliography.

It will have been observed that to Liu Hsiang [37] was entrusted the examination of all those classes of litera-

---

of the Commercial Press, Shanghai. The translation of the first twelve chapters of the *Tsien Han shu* has been made by H. H. Dubs, *The History of the Former Han Dynasty*, 5 volumes (Baltimore, 1938–).

[36] The Chinese is 條其篇目 *tiao chi pien mu*, which is here translated literally. Legge's free version "arranged the contents" suggests the kind of editorial activity with which Kang Yu-wei has taxed Liu Hsiang's son, unjustly, as has already been observed (cf. *supra*, this chap., n. 28).

[37] 79–8 B.C. Considerable discussion has centered about the dating of this important scholar's career. His biography in the "History of the Former Han," XXXVI (no. 4), 6b3–33b9, closes with the cryptic statements, "He died at 72. Thirteen years after his death Wang [Mang] displaced (代) the Han." The puzzle lies

ture which fall within the purview of a liberal human-
istic culture. The three men assigned to help him were
specialists in diverse branches of the science of the time.
It is plain that the condensed "Seven Summaries" of

in identification of this last event. Several writers have supposed
that the assumption by Wang Mang of the imperial title 新皇帝
Sin Huang Di or "Emperor of the Sin Dynasty," in the last month
of A.D. 8, is the point of departure for calculating Liu Hsiang's dates.
These are accordingly stated as 77–6 B.C. by 吳修 Wu Hsiu in the
續疑年錄 *Sü i nien lu*, by 葉德輝 Yeh De-hui in his 前漢書補注
Tsien Han Shu bu ju, and by 梅毓 Mei Yü in his 劉更生年表
Liu Geng-sheng nien biao in the 積學齋叢書 *Dzi Hsüeh Jai tsung
shu*. Pelliot seems to incline to their verdict in his review of Courant's *Catalogue*, no. 3481, BEFEO, III, 721. The same dates are
given, with an alternative citation, in 張惟驤 Jang Wei-rang's
疑年錄彙編 *I nien lu hui bien*, I, 3b; and, without the alternative,
in 梁廷燦 Liang Ting-tsan's recent (1933) 歷代名人生卒年表
Li-dai ming-ren sheng-dzu nien-biao, p. 4.

That the dates 77–6 B.C. are incorrect is proved by a passage in
the 禮樂志 *Li yüeh jir*, "Essay on Ritual and Music" in the
"History of the Former Han," XXII, 5b7–6b7, which makes it
clear that Liu Hsiang died during consideration by the ministers of
state of his proposal for establishment of a 辟雍 *bi yung*, insular
hall for classical exposition, in imitation of Jou precedent. The
proposal was accepted, but before the hall could be completed the
Emperor Cheng died, in the 3d month of 7 B.C. The indicated date,
8 B.C., for the death of Liu Hsiang, is confirmed by the fact that
thirteen years later, A.D. 6, is the first during which Wang Mang
actually exercised imperial power, even performing the distinctively
imperial rites of suburban sacrifice at the altar of Heaven. The
dates 79–8 B.C. have been supported by 錢大昕 Tsien Da-sin in
his 前漢書補注 *Tsien Han Shu bu ju*; by 吳榮光 Wu Rung-
guang in his 歷代名人年譜 *Li-dai ming-ren nien-pu*; and, with
full discussion, by 錢穆 Tsien Mu in a long article 劉向歆父子
年譜 *Liu Hsiang Hsin fu dz nien-pu*, 燕京學報 *Yenching Journal*,
VII (June 1930), 1189–1318, esp. 1193–94, 1231–32, 1270–71.
They are now well established.

In a still more recent article, 劉向之生卒及其撰著考略 *Liu
Hsiang jir sheng-dzu ji chi juan-ju kao-lüeh*, 史學年報 *Yenching*

Liu Hsin [38] were digested directly from the abstracts of his father. It is clear also that the historian Ban Gu has based his "Essay on Literature" directly upon the "Seven Summaries." The latter fact is proved not only by his concluding statement quoted above, but also by his careful indication, in connection with the text itself, of those few items which he personally has added. It is even probable that the labors of the two Liu, father and

---

Annual of Historical Studies, I, no. 5 (1933), 53–60, esp. 53–55, 葛啓揚 Go Chi-yang has attempted to show that the true dates are 80–9 B.C., indicated in Giles, *Biographical Dictionary*, no. 1300. He points out that Liu Hsiang received his first official post upon reaching manhood (the Chinese age of twenty), and that one of his associates was thereafter sent on a special mission apparently in the year 61 B.C. But we have no certain evidence that Liu did not receive his appointment at nineteen, that he actually served with the envoy, or that the mission may not have taken place in 60 B.C. In support of his thesis Go points out that the death of 平帝 the Emperor Ping took place on the 16th of the 12th month of the year roughly corresponding to A.D. 5. Thus Ban Gu might have meant this year in his statement about Wang's displacement of the Han. Against this view must be cited the facts that only two weeks of that year remained, that much of that short period must have been occupied in the negotiations with the dowager-empress, and that Wang's assumption of the 居攝 *jü she*, "protectorate," dates only from the beginning of the next year. It is not probable that Ban, writing seventy years later, had in mind the few days of informal protectorate at the close of A.D. 5.

[38] *Ca.* 46 B.C.–A.D. 23. His biography in the "History of the Former Han," XXXVI (no. 5), 33b10–38a9, has been translated by E. J. Eitel, *China Review*, XV (1886–87), 90–95. A large amount of collateral information has been assembled by Tsien Mu in the article cited in the preceding note. Liu Hsin, as a youth of exceptional attainments (fifteen ?, Chinese reckoning), was presented in 32 B.C. to the new Emperor Cheng, who was then himself of that age. Tsien, *Yenching Journal*, VII, 1213–14. A decade later he served with Wang Mang, who was born in 45 B.C. *Ibid.*, 1209, 1219–20.

son, served to suggest to him the desirability of making literature the subject of a special essay, a procedure which was at that time without any other precedent.[39]

Liu Hsiang's tabulations and extracts are now unfortunately lost; but they continued to circulate at least

[39] Similarly, it is probable that he was led to include in his history another innovation, the 五行志 Wu hsing jir, "Essay on the Five Elements," by the fact that the materials were ready to hand in compilations of 董仲舒 Dung Jung-shu and Liu Hsiang. With regard to the former, cf. Woo Kang, Les trois théories politiques, pp. 18–19, 23–24. The "History of the Former Han," XXXVI (no. 4), 21b8–9, 22a1, relates that when Liu Hsiang was first given charge of collation of the five classics and of the imperial private library he perceived that in the 尙書洪範 Hung Fan section of the "Canon of History" 箕子 Philosopher Ji replies to 武王 Wu Wang (founder of the Jou dynasty) by setting forth the five elements, the positive and negative principles, good fortune and calamity. He himself thereupon compiled a record of auspicious events and calamities from high antiquity to the Tsin and Han. This work is cited as the 劉向五行傳記 Liu Hsiang wu hsing juan ji, 11 rolls, in the Han "Essay on Literature," XXX, 4a2; and under slightly varied titles with the same volume in the corresponding essays of the standard 隋書 "Sui History," XXXII, 11a2–3, 舊唐書 "Old Tang History," XLVI, 9a5, and 新唐書 "New Tang History," LVII, 5a10.

Maspero has pointed out (BEFEO, IX [1909], 595, n. 1) that all the end of the 地理志 Di li jir, "Essay on Geography" in the "History of the Former Han," XXVIII, sec. 2, is in reality a work of Liu Hsiang on geographical divisions, composed after 32 B.C., with additions on habits and customs by another hand. De Saussure (JA, CCIII [1923], 360–362) remarks that Ban Gu in the 律歷志 Lü li jir, "Essay on Measurement and Chronology," in the same work, XXI, sec. 2, 21b10–22b1, explains the (illusory) system by which he has calculated the chronology of ancient times, avowedly following the theory advocated by Liu Hsin in his treatise, 三統 San tung, "The Three Epochs." 范文瀾 Fan Wen-lan, moreover, in his 正史考略 Jeng shir kao lüeh, "Epitome of Studies on the Standard Histories," p. 31, states that Ban Gu, for his 禮樂志 Li yüeh jir, "Essay on Ritual and Music," draws chiefly on the writ-

until the Tang dynasty (618–907) [40] and are in small
part known to us through early citations.[41] Liu Hsin's
"Seven Summaries," too, were independently transmitted to the same period,[42] although it appears that
Ban Gu had reproduced virtually the whole of six of
them, rejecting, perhaps as too diffuse, only the intro-
ductory "General Summary." [43]

The significance of these bibliographic labors is not
easily exaggerated, for they resulted in production of a
nearly complete inventory of books in circulation at
about the opening of the Christian Era, with notes on
their earlier transmission — a document which enables
us to trace with assurance to ancient times the early
texts that are still current, which helps us to confound
the incompetent forger, and which reveals to us the
extent of our literary loss. The importance of insertion
of this bibliography in Ban Gu's great history, the

ings of four men, among them Liu Hsiang. It thus appears that the
ideas, and in large degree the very language, of the two Liu play a
conspicuous part in five of the nine essays of the first truly dynastic
history.

[40] Probably at first known simply as 別錄 *Bieh lu*, "Separate
Records," these are cited as the 七略 *Tsi lüeh bieh lu*, or "Separate
Records of the Seven Summaries, 20 rolls, by Liu Hsiang," in the
essays on literature in the "Sui History," XXXIII, 28a10, and the
"Old" and "New Tang Histories," XLVI, 42b6, and LVIII, 27b6,
respectively.

[41] A chapter of fragments has been gathered by 馬國翰 Ma
Guo-han under the title *Tsi lüeh bieh lu* in his 玉函山房所輯佚書
Yü Han Shan Fang so dzi i shu (1883), vol. 64.

[42] The citation, *Tsi lüeh*, "Seven Summaries, 7 rolls, by Liu
Hsin," follows that of the "Separate Records" in each of the three
standard essays cited in n. 40.

[43] Fragments of this first summary are united by 顧實 Gu Shir
in his study 漢書藝文志講疏 *Han shu I wen jir jiang su* (Shanghai [1924], 1933), pp. 1–13.

second in the form which was later accorded official recognition as standard, and the first to be consecrated to a single dynasty, is accentuated by the fact that it thus established a precedent for later writers of standard history to follow.

For six hundred years no historian ventured to accept the challenge to register the whole written heritage of his time. Finally, in the seventh century, with the strong Tang dynasty upon the throne, an "Essay on Literature" was prepared under the auspices of an imperial commission, to accompany the standard histories of five lesser dynasties. That essay is now appended to the "History of the Sui." [44] Similar essays were in time compiled for both "Old" [45] and "New Tang Histories." [46]

All of the four bibliographies which have just been mentioned are alike in essential character. Each aims to record all extant serious literature, irrespective of the time of production. Each presents a series of classified lists identified by suitable rubrics. For each indi-

---

[44] 隋書 *Sui shu*, XXXII–XXXV, 2 volumes. It is entitled 經籍志 *Jing ji jir*. As Fan Wen-lan ("Epitome of Studies on the Standard Histories," p. 139) points out, the strength of the Tang scholars lies rather in polite letters than in classical studies. For the history of early texts this essay is much less reliable than the one in the *Han shu*; but it is still invaluable as a contemporary record of their preservation in the medieval period, and for the light it sheds on the literature of the intervening six centuries.

[45] 舊唐書 *Jiu Tang shu*, XLVI–XLVII, 1 volume. It is also entitled *Jing ji jir*.

[46] 新唐書 *Sin Tang shu*, LVII–LX, 1 volume. The title is again *I wen jir* as in the *Han shu*. It should be noted that, although the "New Tang History" was compiled in the eleventh century, the essay cites only books current in Tang times, some of which had doubtless meantime disappeared from circulation.

vidual book are cited the title, textual or physical division, and author. In the Han and Sui histories each major group of works is accompanied by a special disquisition on the circumstances of composition, and textual history of its chief components. Doubtless because of the progressive expansion of the national literature, in the two Tang histories this supplementary information is reduced to a minimum.

With the effective introduction and perfection of block printing from the tenth to the thirteenth centuries,[47] the volume of literature in circulation swelled enormously, the danger of disappearance of valuable works was vastly reduced, and it became of paramount importance to identify editions. Largely as result of these changed conditions, although essays on literature continued to find a place in successive later standard histories, their importance has paled beside the rich independent bibliographic literature produced by Chinese critical scholars and bibliophiles of the last three centuries. How fully this literature permits control of transmission of the rarer editions and manuscripts (which of course have received special attention) may be illustrated by the genealogical tree on pages 42–43, which represents the ancestry of part of the books now in the National Library in Peking [48] and of a large portion

[47] T. F. Carter, *The Invention of Printing in China and Its Spread Westward* (2nd ed., New York, 1931), pp. 47–69.

[48] The diagram of immediate antecedents of the library is based on data presented by Léonard Aurousseau, BEFEO, XII, no. 9 (1912), 63–79, in his review of 繆荃孫 Miao Tsüan-sun's catalogue of rarities in the old Library of the Ministry of Education, which was founded in 1909, and renamed in 1912 the 京師圖書館 Metropolitan Library. Most of those rarities were derived from the rich 內閣 Cabinet Library, with purchases from the private libraries

of the Seikadō Bunko of Baron Iwasaki Koyata, one
of the richest Chinese libraries in Japan.⁴⁹

It will of course be evident that continuity of record
affords a valuable control, although not in itself a proof,
of authenticity.⁵⁰ On the negative side, the argument
from silence can hardly be invoked with telling effect
if a work is shown to be missing from but one of the

---

of the Yao and Chü families. The 國子監 National College con-
tributed modern editions. The best extant copy of the manuscript
四庫全書 *Sz ku tsüan shu*, "Complete Work of the Four Treasuries" in 36,300 volumes, was added from the 避暑山莊 Bi Shu
Shan Juang at 熱河 Rir Ho (Jehol); as were also 8,000 rolls of early
manuscript Buddhist sūtras discovered on the confines of East
Turkestan (cf. *infra*, p. 45). The China Foundation for the Promo-
tion of Education and Culture, which is endowed with the second
remitted portion of the American share in the Boxer Indemnity,
established in 1926 a new Metropolitan Library (北海圖書館
literally "North Sea Library") of which the collection was consciously destined to supplement those of the senior institution, with
which it was united in 1929 as the National Library. Its history is
traced by Director 袁同禮 T. L. Yüan, in charge since 1926,
Annual Report (1930), pp. 1–4.

⁴⁹ It was purchased in 1907 from the heirs of Lu Sin-yüan, who
had made systematic efforts to collect the best portions of the
libraries scattered by the Tai Ping rebellion. Pelliot, "L'oeuvre de
Lou Sin-yuan," BEFEO, IX (1909), 211–249, 427–469, esp. 427–
428, 464–467. The famous catalogue of Lu's rarities, 皕宋樓藏
書志 *Bi Sung Lou tsang shu jir* (1882), 124 chapters, 40 volumes,
is supplemented by the 靜嘉堂秘籍志 *Seikadō hisekishi* (1917),
50 chapters, 25 volumes. Pelliot traces the history of the collection
to the Shir Li Jü; and Aurousseau (BEFEO, XII, no. 9 [1912], 98)
outlines the sources of that library. For the biography of Tsien
Chien-i and the fortunes of another portion of his library, cf. L. C.
Goodrich, *The Literary Inquisition of Ch'ien-lung* (Baltimore, 1935),
pp. 100–107, esp. n. 7.

⁵⁰ Karlgren (Ancient Texts, BMFEA, I, 167–168, criterion no. 6)
has cited the instances of the "early" 關尹子 *Guan Yin Dz* and
亢倉子 *Kang Tsang Dz*, the first of which is probably, the latter
certainly, a forgery.

early essays and is still mentioned in both earlier and later documents, for the compilers of those essays were apt to err by omission. Especially is this true during the later epochs, when books were no longer scarce.

Attention should be drawn to the importance of the records of textual division,[51] for the textual division of a Chinese — as of a Western — book is normally dictated by the development of the subject. Any alteration in such division must ordinarily reflect either omission of some part of the original text, addition to it, or a complete recasting of the former treatment of the subject. This is true whether there be involved an early book or a more modern one. The former was originally divided by its author, or perhaps an editor of the Han period, into (usually short) subject-sections called 篇 *pien*, and was then or later inscribed on one or more rolls 卷 *jüan* of silk, silk floss paper, or vegetable fiber paper (as these materials were successively adopted) at the convenience of the scribe, as dictated by considerations of cost, or depending on inclusion or exclusion of comment. With introduction of printing and of the stitched book, it was found feasible to reproduce the matter of more than one roll within the compass of a volume, 本 *ben* or 冊 *tse*, and the old term for a roll, *jüan*, acquired new meaning as a structural division of the text by subject, approximately equivalent to our Western chapter. It follows that an alteration in the number of *jüan*, rolls, of an ancient text or of *ben*, volumes, of a modern one, both merely physical divisions, is a matter of indifference; but that altera-

[51] Maspero has stressed this matter in his review of Karlgren's Ancient Texts (criterion no. 7), JA, vol. CCXXII (1933), "Bulletin critique," pp. 41–42.

THE FILIATION OF MODERN CHINESE LIBRARIES

匪載閣
Fei Dzai Go
of
劉子威
Liu Dz-wei

懸罄室
Hsüan Ching Shir
of
錢叔寶
Tsien Shu-bao

七檜山房
Tsi Kuei Shan Fang
of
楊儀 (玉川)
Yang I (Wu-chuan)

二世脈望館
Er Shir Mo Wang Guan
of
趙汝師
Jao Ru-shir

絳雲
Jiang Yün
of
錢謙益
Tsien Chien-i
1582 — 1664

Dispersion

士禮居
Shir Li Ju
of
黃丕烈
Huang Pei-lieh
1763–1825

水月月亭
Shui Yüeh Ting
of
周錫瓚
Jou Si-dzan

五研樓
Wu Yen Lou
of
袁廷檮
Yüan Ting-tao

小讀書堆
Siao Du Shu Dui
of
顧之逵
Gu Jir-kuei

藝芸
I Yün
of
汪士鐘 (閬源)
Wang Shir-jung (Lang-yüan)

?

?

鐵琴銅劍樓
Tieh Chin Tung Jien Lou
of
瞿氏
Chü family

海源閣
Hai Yüan Go
of
楊氏
Yang family

宜稼堂
I Jia Tang
of
郁松年
Yu Sung-nien

皕宋樓
Bi Sung Lou
and
十萬卷樓
Shir Wan Jüan Lou
of
陸心源
Lu Sin-yüan
d. 1894

靜嘉堂文庫
Seikadō Bunko
1907
of
岩崎小彌太
Iwasaki Koyata

持靜齋
Chir Jing Jai
of
丁日昌
Ding Rir-chang

莫友芝
Mo Yu-jir

洪氏
Mr. Hung

避暑山莊
Bi Shu Shan Juang

國子監
Guo Dz Jien

敦煌
Dun Huang

跂進齋
Jir Dzin Jai
of
姚氏
Yao family

內閣
Nei Go

學部圖書館
Hsüeh Bu Tu-shu-guan (1909)

京師圖書館
Jing Shir Tu-shu-guan (1912)

北海圖書館
Bei Hai Tu-shu-guan (1926)

北海圖書館
Bei Hai Tu-shu-guan (1929)

國立北平圖書館
Guo-li Bei Ping Tu-shu-guan

tion in the number of *pien*, sections, in an ancient text, or of *jüan*, now chapters, in a modern one, both of which are subject divisions, is on the contrary a matter of grave concern.

Respect for established texts and scrupulous fidelity in their reproduction (in intent at least) are among the most conspicuous and meritorious characteristics of Chinese scholarship. If, then, we detect a variation in the textual division of a Chinese work in the history of its transmission, it behooves us to inquire carefully for an explanation. Diminution can often be accounted for by loss. Augmentation is, *prima facie*, more serious. In the case of an early work it inevitably provokes (sometimes unfounded) suspicion of forgery. In that of a modern one it suggests addition or, more rarely, recasting; in any event, a new edition.

The fortunate circumstance of archaeological discovery permits external control of many texts. Reference has already been made [52] to the opening in A.D. 281 of a tomb which appears to have been sealed shortly after 299 B.C. In the tomb were found bamboo manuscripts from which the highly competent scholars of the time were able to decipher, in part at least, the text of fifteen works, most notably the "Annals Written on Bamboo" and the "Romance of Mu, Son of Heaven." [53]

[52] *Supra*, p. 7. Cf., especially, Chavannes, *Mémoires historiques*, V, 451–465.

[53] 穆天子傳 *Mu Tien-Dz juan*. English translation by E. J. Eitel, *China Review*, XVII (1888–89), 223–240, 247–258. Chavannes (*Mémoires historiques*, II, 5–8) points out that this work and the third chapter of 列子 *Lieh Dz*, which seems to reproduce part of it, are the chief early sources for the king's legendary journey to the west which in its early form features especially his marvelous coursers, capable of a thousand *li* (300 miles) a day. He translates the laconic narrative of the "Annals Written on Bamboo," which, like

Obviously, neither of these works can have been forged in the period of nearly six centuries during which the tomb was closed. Nor is the silence of Han literature concerning them any occasion for suspicion.

The classic triumph of modern archaeology in Central Asia is the recovery for science intact, with but negligible exceptions, of a rich deposit of manuscripts which had been walled up for protection from the Tangutans in a cave temple near Dun Huang about A.D. 1000.[54] The library was discovered by accident in 1900, but fortunately only a few samples were extracted and scattered. Late in 1907 Sir Aurel Stein was able to secure for the British Museum a selection of manuscripts [55] in the languages of Central Asia; and a few

---

the other early versions, mentions 西王母 Si-wang-mu with the apparent implication that this personage was a male chieftain of the western frontier. Latest champion of this view is W. P. Yetts, *Catalogue of the Eumorfopoulos Collection, Bronzes*, II (London, 1930), 39. At least in later mythology the Si Wang Mu is the Queen Mother of the West, in whose garden grow the peaches of immortality. Maspero identifies her as a primitive goddess of epidemics, while Pelliot now regards her as a very ancient mythological personage, always feminine. TP, XXVII (1930), 392. An attempted identification with the Queen of Sheba has not been generally accepted. A. Forke, "Mu Wang und die Königin von Saba," *Mitteilungon des Seminars für Orientalische Sprachen* (Berlin), VII (1904), 117–172; reviewed by Edouard Huber, BEFEO, IV (1904), 1127–31. Cf. review of this work and H. A. Giles' identification of Si-wang-mu as Juno, by Pelliot, BEFEO, VI (1906), 416–421.

[54] 敦煌 Dun Huang in western Gansu province was prior to that time the point of bifurcation of the northern and southern trade routes to Turkestan and western Asia which passed either side of the Taklamakan desert. The latest dates found on documents from this hoard are those of the 至道 Jir-Dao reign period, 995–997. See note of the present writer, *Harvard Journal of Asiatic Studies*, I (1936), 271.

[55] M. A. Stein, *Ruins of Desert Cathay* (London, 1912), I, 166–194, 211–219, esp. 217–218.

months later Paul Pelliot sorted out for the Bibliothèque Nationale those which remained, and the most
interesting of those in Chinese.[56] In passing through
Peking, moreover, Pelliot succeeded in persuading the
Chinese government to complete the rescue of all that
remained of the deposit, some 8,000 manuscripts.[57]

The archaeological discoveries just mentioned have
been fortunately supplemented by identification of
numerous early editions and manuscripts, some of the
latter even of Tang date, which have been preserved
in Japan. Many significant documents have been
recovered from this source, which began to be tapped
almost immediately when the Chinese government
sent diplomatic envoys — who were also scholars —
to Tōkyō. The first collection was published there by
one of these in 1884.[58] Since that time other series have
been issued by Chinese and Japanese alike.[59] The

[56] Paul Pelliot, "Une bibliothèque médiévale retrouvée au Kan-
sou," BEFEO, VIII (1908), 501–529. Concrete illustrations of the
importance of these finds are provided by Pelliot, "Le Chou King
en caractères anciens," part 2, MAO, II (1916), 135–177, pl. 20–26.

[57] Léonard Aurousseau, review of inventory of them by 李翊灼
Li I-shao, BEFEO, XII, no. 9 (1912), 88–89.

[58] The 古逸叢書 Gu i tsung shu, 49 volumes, edited by 黎庶昌
Li Shu-chang. The whole collection has been analyzed by Pelliot,
BEFEO, II (1902), 315–340.

[59] The Shanghai Commercial Press has issued 46 volumes of a
supplement to Li Shu-chang's work, entitled 續古逸叢書 Sü gu
i tsung shu. Additional volumes are issued from time to time.

Some of the earlier Japanese publications of medieval Chinese
texts are noticed by Chavannes, TP, XIII (1912), 482–507; and by
Pelliot, TP, XXIII (1924), 15–30. Since 1925 the lead in such publication has been taken by the 東洋文庫 Tōyō Bunko or Oriental
Library of Baron 岩崎久彌 Iwasaki Hisaya. Cf. reviews of Maspero, JA, CCXII (1928), 165–170; and Pelliot, TP, XXVI (1929),
357–366.

manuscripts secured in this manner, whether from Dun Huang or from Japan, afford an invaluable control over many subsequent editions, not only directly through the texts which they reproduce, but through the examples of early paleography which they present to the textual critic.

It has been remarked that Chinese scholars have shown exemplary respect for established texts. In perhaps no other literature is the establishment of texts a more essential preliminary to their historical utilization. The peculiar necessity for textual criticism arises not so much from the long period through which many texts have been transmitted (those of ancient Greece can boast as great antiquity), but rather from the extraordinary ease with which they can be — and have been — altered.

In considering the alteration of Chinese texts it is well to bear in mind the method of block printing which has been most in favor and most widely used from the tenth century until our own. The text to be printed is written by a professional scribe in formal characters upon broad sheets of thin paper which are ruled in vertical columns, ordinarily eighteen to twenty-six in number, with a distinctive center column designed to receive the title of the work, with the chapter and page numbers. Each sheet is then pasted, inverted, upon a smooth block of pear wood, and skilled carvers cut away the background of the characters and column-ruling so that these stand in relief. Ink is brushed vertically across the surface, a sheet of paper is laid upon it, and impression is assured by deft brushing of the back. Each sheet is printed on one side only and is

then folded down the center column so that the index-
ing which it bears is partly visible from either side.
The loose edges of the folio are then stitched with
eighty to one hundred and fifty others to form a limp
paper-covered volume.

It will be observed that this process of printing
involves the direct reproduction of a manuscript copy,
as does also the modern and cheaper lithographic
process. Wood blocks from which prints have been
taken in sufficient quantity are ordinarily scraped
smooth to receive another text; but in the case of
especially valuable works, and those published by
imperial [60] or provincial authority, the blocks were
placed in storage so that additional impressions might
be taken to meet future needs. Through the vicissi-

[60] W. F. Mayers ("Bibliography of the Chinese Imperial Collections of Literature," *China Review*, VI [1877–1878], 294–295) calls
attention to an estimate of cost in 1773 for printing an imperial
wood-block edition of Sz-ma Tsien's "Historical Memoirs." The
cost is stated at 1,447.5 taels or ounces of silver (representing a
purchasing power somewhat in excess of that of American dollars):
2,675 blocks at 1/10 tael, plus engraving of 1,189,000 characters at
1/10 tael per 100. This estimate is higher than the cost of a similar
edition to a private publishing house or individual, for in China
prices are normally adapted to the financial status of the purchaser,
and the emperor is better able to pay than any of his subjects. This
cost for a single edition is contrasted with an estimate of only 1,200
taels for a fount of 100,000 large movable wooden type, and 50,000
small ones for commentary at 8/10 tael per 100. These estimates
were presented by 金簡 Jin Jien to the emperor and accepted by
him. The type cut by his order was employed to print 138 of the
most valuable works which had been accepted for inclusion in the
great manuscript "Complete Work of the Four Treasuries." The
print and method of its execution with the type, called "assembled
gems" by the emperor, are fully illustrated by Jin Jien in the 武英
殿聚珍版程式 *Wu Ying Dien jü jen ban cheng shir*, published in
1776 with, as preface, the memorial presenting the estimates.

tudes of printing and storage the blocks become worn
and damaged, sometimes split, perhaps some of them
lost altogether. For later printings, damaged blocks
are repaired so far as possible and new ones cut to make
up deficiencies. The best quality of paper and the most
careful workmanship are naturally expended upon the
earliest prints, while the blocks are in perfect condition.
Later, inferior paper and careless printing are apt to
be considered good enough for badly worn or damaged
blocks. Characters may be obscured by folds, defects,
or even small holes in the paper; cracks are reflected
by black lines athwart the page; while whole pages
may be rendered nearly or in part illegible through
slight shifting of the paper on the block. Sometimes
pages are so badly smudged that a later owner will
have the text restored by collation with a better copy,
in red manuscript upon the blackened ground.

It should be remembered also that classical written
Chinese is an uninflected monosyllabic language of
which one of the most distinctive features is the flexi-
bility that permits many words to serve at will in various capacities, as different parts of speech. Whether a
given term represents a noun, adjective, or verb depends
primarily on position. Auxiliary connectives are used
but sparingly. It will then readily be grasped that it is
not always easy to see at a glance that a given sentence
lacks any specific element; and that a scribe whose
training lies rather in calligraphy than in scholarship
understands the texts which flow from his brush even
less than does the Western typist. A further difficulty
lies in the latitude of personal idiosyncrasy which is
permissible in cursive writing. Probably writers in

every land tend to trespass on the margin of legibility. Precisely because Chinese characters are individually more distinctive to the eye than words written in alphabetic script, it is possible to suggest them in a greater variety of ways. Abbreviation is, to be sure, guided by the different examples set by past masters of calligraphy, whose models are in the hands of every school boy; but each scholar is free to develop his own eclectic style.[61] Recognition of characters which are rather indicated than explicitly inscribed is often possible only through comprehension of the context.

Simple errors of reading are responsible for not a few textual alterations. Even a careful copyist or typesetter may make mistakes if compelled to work from a cursive manuscript, from a late print from broken or badly worn blocks, or from one which has been carelessly smudged. Sometimes a text is dilapidated: badly torn or worn with much handling, as is often the case with the beginning of medieval rolls, or it may be rendered largely illegible by the ravages of the book worm.[62]

[61] The most influential of the early masters, examples of whose work is preserved by inscription on stone, is 王羲之 Wang Hsi-jir, A.D. 321–379. Giles, *Biographical Dictionary*, no. 2174. Reproduction by rubbing from stone inscriptions was practised centuries before application of block printing to books. Carter, *The Invention of Printing in China*, pp. 12–16, 197–199. The 名人草字彙 *Ming ren tsao dz hui*, "Repertory of Grass Characters by Famous Men," compiled in 1787 by 堅菴 Shu An in 6 slim volumes, is a dictionary of various cursive forms employed by 87 noted calligraphers.

[62] The book worm thrives with dampness, which is greatly promoted by failure of the Chinese to use a dry course in building the tamped mud walls of their houses. It is largely for this reason that wealthy owners of libraries prefer to house them in upper pavilions or 樓 *lou*. Fortunately, rare items are usually protected against worms by casing in camphor wood.

A second group of alterations results from choice by editor or copyist. A character may be replaced by an authorized or unauthorized variant, or by another character of similar sound or appearance, either through an effort at modernization, intent to avoid a form which is temporarily taboo because it occurs in the personal name of an emperor of the reigning dynasty, or simply through preference for another form as habitual, quicker to write, or more beautiful. Whenever a typesetter encounters a character which is lacking from his fount, there is inevitable temptation to substitution.

Unconscious alterations in reproduction are not uncommon. Additions to a text, as already seen, may result from incorporation of interlinear comment. Omission in copy is much more frequent, extending usually to only a single character, but sometimes to a phrase, column, or whole passage. Omission of part of a page which has failed to receive impression is customarily made up in manuscript by collation. The same practice is followed to complete a work of which a page or more may have been omitted by the binder. Missing or displaced pages are indeed so common that good library accession practice calls for comprehensive inspection of the marginal paging. Alteration in very early texts has in some cases resulted from incorrect assemblage of bamboo slips when their binding thongs were broken. Particularly numerous errors result from mistakes in typography: identification of complex characters in reverse on small type is not easy. Another group of changes springs from phonetic confusion, substitution of a homonym in a passage carried in the head of a copyist or of a scholar. Reliance on memory for quotation is a fruitful source of variants. A natural corollary of ease of alteration of texts is emphasis upon careful proofing. Good scholars often serve their friends as proofreaders, and their names are honorably inscribed as such side by side with those of the authors.

A garbled text can often be detected by a competent scholar, but reconstruction of the original wording is by no means always possible. Collation of variant readings is of course the primary method for establishing a text. In Chinese, even more often than in Western literature, an entire family of identical readings may spring from a common source, so that it is quite essential to determine independence of evidence admitted. Collation is greatly facilitated by the elaborate exegetical compilations of the Manchu period. In cases of evident alteration when no useful variant is available, final resort is had to conjectural emendation. As always, this delicate task requires familiarity with the hazards to which texts are exposed and, above all, with the particular language appropriate to the one in question. How serious this linguistic preparation may be in the case of the earliest documents is suggested by the declaration of Wang Guo-wei,[63] one of the greatest contemporary scholars, that in a large number of passages the "Canon of History" is unintelligible.

Interpretation of meaning is evidently a prerequisite of intelligent emendation. As already stated, the Chinese language has evolved surely if slowly from age

---

[63] 王國維 1877–1927. Pelliot, obituary notice, TP, XXVI (1928–29), 70–72; "L'édition collective des oeuvres de Wang Kouo-wei," TP, XXVI, 113–182. For the statement here cited, cf. TP, XXIX (1932), 207.

to age, with the progressive creation of new words and
new forms of expression to convey new thoughts. Only,
unlike the situation in western lands, this evolution
has proceeded without a break, continuity of literary
tradition closely linking the best products of each
epoch. Thus, when the school boy of today seeks his
models of expression, he finds those for ethical writing
among the philosophers of the fifth to the third centuries B.C., history in the great Han works of Sz-ma
Tsien and Ban Gu, poetry in the Tang, essays in the
Sung, drama in the Yüan, and novels in the Ming. All
worthy literary forms have been objects of emulation
in all subsequent periods, so that modern Chinese
literature is extraordinarily varied. Individual words,
in acquiring new acceptances, have not relinquished
the old ones. And whole series of compound expressions have been stereotyped to provide special technical
vocabularies without increasing the number of characters [64] in use. Thanks to the Chinese' love of pithy
expression and to their strong antiquarian bent, felici-
tous phraseology and concise formulae have been

---

[64] H. A. Giles' *Chinese-English Dictionary* contains virtually all
characters in accepted usage, under 13,848 entries, about one-fifth
of which represent variant readings. Mr. Giles in 1924 stated to the
writer his belief that a well-educated Chinese recognizes about 6,000
characters. This estimate agrees well with the statement by 金簡
Jin Jien in 1773 (cf. *supra*, n. 60) that he had found 6,500 characters
in common use in the great thesaurus of literary allusion, 佩文韻府
Pei wen yün fu. The number of words — recognized symbols for
ideas — in the language, is vastly greater. The true difficulty in
learning Chinese resides in recognition, not of characters themselves,
but of their specific meaning as indicated by their position and
context. Karlgren, *Sound and Symbol in Chinese* (London, 1923),
40, 84–98.

amassed in ever swelling volume. Oblique senses, too, and allusion are met with even in official documents, for in China, at least since the seventh century, every official is assumed to be a classical scholar, and the public to whom state papers were addressed could be expected to understand and appreciate them.

External evidence affords final proof that even the best efforts of excellent Chinese scholars armed with the weapons of collation and emendation have not sufficed to preserve even important documents from alteration. This appears already from the diversity of versions of standard works now current. Among early texts found in Japan is a fragmentary Tang manuscript of the "Essay on Economics" in the "History of the Former Han," a work which has been widely read and respected ever since its compilation. One hundred characters are found to differ from those of the consecrated modern text.[65] Enough has perhaps been said about the alteration of Chinese texts to make clear that no conscientious scholar will willingly base his work upon an inferior edition if it is possible for him to gain access to a better one.

The normal ease of alteration of Chinese texts was of necessity greatly accentuated in the first centuries before Christ, when the very characters of the language and the materials for writing it were being subjected to comprehensive modification, and when for a score of years a large proportion of all literature was proscribed. It is not surprising that afterward, when learning again found favor at the now truly imperial court,

---

[65] Pelliot, "Notes de bibliographie chinoise, I, Le *Kou yi ts'ung chou*," BEFEO, II (1902), 315–340, esp. 335.

it was discovered that many ancient texts were current in sharply divergent recensions. Of the "Odes" there were no fewer than four versions, representing as many schools of interpretation.[66] Three schools with divergent texts professed to interpret the "Spring and Autumn

[66] The 魯 Lu version of the 詩 *Shir* "Odes" or *Lu shir*, was first taught at the capital by 申公 the Hon. Shen, who was appointed 博士 Bo Shir, or Professor, by 文帝 the Emperor Wen (179–157 B.C.), and who resigned in 162 to return to his native Shandung (Lu) with a pupil who had been named 楚王 Prince of Chu. He was succeeded in office by more than ten disciples as also by his son and grandson during the next twenty-five years. Maspero, "La Composition," MCB, I, 195–196; Karlgren, Early History, BMFEA, III, 17. The 韓 Han school was likewise recognized at court, where its chief exponent 韓嬰 Han Ying, whose doctrine was popular in 燕 Yen and 趙 Jao (the northeast), was also appointed Bo Shir by Emperor Wen, promoted by his successor, and called to debate before 武帝 the Emperor Wu (140–87) against the great scholar 董仲舒 Dung Jung-shu. The third school, that of 齊 Tsi, was headed by 轅固 Yüan Gu, who was appointed Professor of the Odes by 景帝 the Emperor Jing (156–141). These three recensions with their respective commentaries, among which that of Han differed sharply from the others, were all taught at the capital from this time.

A fourth recension of the Odes had been edited with commentary by 毛亨 Mao Heng and perhaps by 毛萇 Mao Chang as well, and was popular at the court, 155–130, of 河間獻王 Prince Hsien of Ho Jien (the region about the modern prefecture of the same name in present Hobei province). Prince Hsien, however, was unable to secure its official recognition. The 毛詩 or "Odes of Mao" were in fact accepted in the face of opposition from the established schools, only in the period A.D. 1–5 as result of vigorous championship by 劉歆 Liu Hsin; but thereafter they so completely displaced the other versions that these are now preserved only in small part through early citations. Karlgren, BMFEA, III, 12–33. Legge's translation is standard: *The She King or the Book of Poetry* (*Chinese Classics*, IV), 2 vols. (Hongkong, 1871). A fresh translation, independent of traditional interpretation, is that of Arthur Waley, "The Book of Songs" (London, 1937).

Annals" of Confucius.[67] Rival versions of the "Canon of History" provide basis for scholarly controversy to our own day.[68] The great works on ritual also required the editing of Han scholars,[69] as did the ancient

[67] The 春秋 *Chun tsiu*. Two rival ritual commentaries, the 公羊傳 *Gung Yang juan* and 穀梁傳 *Gu Liang juan*, were defended in debate before the Emperor Wu by Dung Jung-shu and 江生 Jiang Sheng, respectively. Woo Kang, *Les trois théories politiques*, pp. 10–14, 28–29, 193–194. Each was accompanied by a recension in modern characters of the classic text. A third small ritual commentary is incorporated into the 左傳 *Dzo juan* (cf. *supra*, chap. II, n. 8), and reproduces fragments of a distinctive (third) recension of the text upon which it was originally based, before Liu Hsin prefixed to it a fresh transcription from a fourth text, in archaic characters, which he found in the imperial library. Maspero ("La Composition," MCB, I, 182–188) concludes that all four recensions derive ultimately from a single text of the "Annals," a defective example presenting mistakes, gaps, inversions of slips, and clumsy attempts at correction of old errors, which are faithfully reproduced in at least the three complete versions.

[68] Cf. *supra*, chap. II, n. 2; and *infra*, p. 61.

[69] The 周禮 *Jou li* "Jou ritual" (or 周官 *Jou guan* "Officers of the Jou," as it was known in Han times) was no doubt already constituted about the fourth century B.C., but was among the works most actively suppressed in 213. Prince Hsien of Ho Jien, who held court 155–130, secured a copy of it in archaic script and presented it to the imperial library, where it remained for a century until Liu Hsin replaced a missing section with another early work, the 考工記 *Kao gung ji*, and published it. Karlgren, Early History, BMFEA, I, 2–8, 35–38, 50–57. Edouard Biot's translation is standard: *Le Tcheou-li ou Rites des Tcheou*, 2 vols. (Paris, 1851).

The ritual which we know as the 儀禮 *I li*, appeared in early Han times in a modern-text version called the 士禮 *Shir li*, or "Ritual of the nobility," in 17 sections, produced by 高堂生 Gao-tang Sheng of 魯 Lu. This version was handed down to 后倉 Hou Tsang, a scholar of the period 73–49, who taught it to three pupils, all of whom secured official scholastic appointments. When in the second century B.C. a group of classical texts in archaic script was discovered in Lu, a scholar named Kung, generally supposed to be 孔安國 Kung An-guo (cf. *supra*, chap. II, n. 2), studied a

divination manual of the Jou dynasty, the "Canon of Change." [70]

Among the many competing texts, some were accorded official recognition at the imperial court of

ritual in 70 sections, found the text agreed well with the version in 17 sections already current, and added 39 sections to it. "History of the Former Han, Essay on Literature," XXX, 7b2–6. The work has been translated by John Steele, *The I-Li or Book of Etiquette and Ceremonial*, 2 vols. (London, 1917), and by Séraphin Couvreur, 儀禮, "Cérémonial" (Hsien Hsien, 1916).

Liu Hsiang, in preparing his full inventory of the imperial library, found a large collection, and four smaller ones, of ritual texts. As listed by his son and recorded in the *Han Shu*, XXX, 6b2–4, 7b10, 11b9, these total 215 sections. All of these texts he grouped under six topical heads, as we know through quotations of his reports by the second-century commentator 鄭玄 Jeng Hsüan, which are in turn cited by the seventh-century commentator 孔穎達 Kung Ying-da. Disappearance of many of these texts is doubtless owing to the efforts of two cousins, 戴德 Dai De and 戴聖 Dai Sheng, both pupils of Hou Tsang, who had shortly before made independent digests or selections from among them, constituting two new collections of more manageable proportions. That of Dai De, now known as the 大戴禮記 *Da Dai li ji*, in 85 sections, divided in modern editions into 13 chapters and 2 volumes, has never been translated. That of Dai Sheng, sometimes distinguished as the 小戴禮記 *Siao Dai li ji*, was already reported by Liu Hsiang under its present ordinary title, "Li ji, 49 sections." It has been translated repeatedly, notably by Legge, *The Li ki (Sacred Books of the East*, XXVII–XXVIII), 2 vols. (Oxford, 1885). Both works and their history are discussed in detail by 梁啓超 Liang Chi-chao in his 要籍解題及其讀法 *Yao-dzi jieh-ti ji chi du-fa* (1925), pp. 165–196, esp. 183–186.

[70] 易經 *I jing* or 周易 *Jou i*, "Changes of the Jou Dynasty." This work, because of its nature, was exempted from destruction in 213. But by the middle of the first century B.C. there were current in the official schools no fewer than five recensions, while two more were being taught without official recognition. It fell to Liu Hsiang to collate four of the official versions with a text in archaic script in the imperial library, and to establish an orthodox text in agreement with one of those theretofore unrecognized. "History of

Chang An,[71] and their interpreters received the title
and emoluments of Professor. The dominant scholar
at court during the first crucial period of selection was
Dung Jung-shu.[72] He it was who in 140 B.C. proposed
establishment of an imperial college and creation of an
educated civil service. He it was who championed the
"Gung Yang Commentary" upon the "Spring and
Autumn Annals," and who through his great influence
largely determined Confucian orthodoxy, new in China.

After foundation of the Grand College in 124 B.C.,
with its rigid scholastic regulations, it was no longer
easy to gain recognition for freshly recovered texts,
however meritorious. This explains why a century
later Liu Hsin felt compelled to wage a violent and
bitter campaign, which was only after apparent defeat
crowned with ultimate victory, to secure official sanction
and adoption of Mao's recension of the "Odes," the
"archaic text" version of the "Canon of History," the
"Jou Ritual," and the "Spring and Autumn Annals"

---

the Former Han," XXX, 3a9–b3. Legge, *The Yî King* (*Sacred
Books*, XVI, Oxford, 1882). Arthur Waley has advanced the plaus-
ible and stimulating thesis that the *I* is a composite work consisting
of a repertory of rustic lore concerning omens, and a more preten-
tious text on divination. "The Book of Changes," BMFEA, V
(1933), 121–142.

[71] 長安, the modern 西安 Si An. Maspero has pointed out that
in the second century B.C. the capital was by no means yet the cultural center which it later became. Nearly all the famous scholars
associated with the early history of famous texts came from the
eastern part of North China. "La Composition," MCB, I, 194–197.

[72] 董仲舒, ca. 175–105 B.C. Woo Kang (*Les trois théories politiques*, pp. 15–33) translates his biography in the "Historical Memoirs," CXXI, utilizing for comment the parallel biography in the
"History of the Former Han," LVI, and some anecdotes from
chap. LXXXVIII of the same work.

with the "Dzo Commentary." The last three were
freshly transcribed from archaic script.

Between A.D. 175 and 183 imperial orders were executed for engraving in stone the complete text of the
classics.[73] This measure did, no doubt, envisage preservation of the canonical works, but it seems that the
leading motive was rather authentication of the texts
selected. In reaction to the former success of the
"archaic text" school represented by Liu Hsin, the
classics to be preserved included, besides the "Canon
of Change," the "Odes," and the "Sayings" of Confucius,[74] the "new text" recension of the "Canon of

[73] 蔡邕 Tsai Yung (133–192; Giles, *Biographical Dictionary*,
no. 1986), to whom the task was entrusted, is reported to have
written the text himself in red ink on stone tablets for the workmen
to cut, and to have fallen victim to a political intrigue shortly after
commencement of the work. The National Library of Beiping has
acquired an oblong fragment measuring 24 × 12 inches, which was
unearthed near 洛陽 Lo Yang in the summer of 1929. The two
faces bear 120 characters beautifully executed in the monumental
隷書 *li shu* "clerkly style." T. L. Yüan, *Annual Report* (1930),
p. 12.

[74] 論語 *Lun yü*, oral traditions of the master's teaching recorded
by his disciples in the third or fourth generation. Among several
translations the most convenient is that of W. E. Soothill, who cites
many variant versions of others, *The Analects of Confucius* (Yoko-
hama, 1910). In A.D. 5 this work was designated with the classics
as a subject for study, and was already so honored by 文帝 the
Emperor Wen (179–157 B.C.), if we can believe 趙岐 Jao Chi of the
second century A.D. Karlgren, Early History, BMFEA, III, 45, 48.

The *Lun yü* was incorporated into the 四書 *Sz shu*, "Four Books,"
as the basis for modern elementary education by 朱熹 Ju Hsi in
the twelfth century. The 大學 *Da hsüeh*, "Great Learning," and
中庸 *Jung yung*, "Invariable Mean," were extracted by him from
the 禮記 *Li ji* "Ritual Records." He included as the fourth work
the 內書 *Nei shu* or personal text of 孟子 Mencius in 7 sections,
ignoring the 4 sections of the 外書 *Wai shu* or supplementary text

History," the *I Li* "Ritual," [75] and the "Spring and Autumn Annals" with the "Gung Yang Commentary." [76]

The triumph of the "modern text" school was premature. In 240-248 the 魏 Wei kingdom, which now occupied the northeastern portion of the former empire, in its turn had two of the classics engraved on stone [77] — the "Spring and Autumn Annals" with the *Dzo Juan*, and the "archaic text" recension of the "Canon of History." The fifteen additional chapters of this last work which had been reconstituted by 孔安國 Kung An-guo [78] early in the first century B.C. were now lost and consequently, of course, not engraved.

---

which had been declared the work of another hand by Jao Chi, and attributed to his disciples by 韓愈 Han Yü (768-824). Maspero gives the history of this last text, JA, vol. CCXXII (1933), "Bulletin critique," pp. 39-40. He has also demonstrated that the whole of Mencius' career now known to us falls within the years 324-314 B.C. TP, XXV (1927-28), 385-386. Legge, *Chinese Classics*: I, *Confucian Analects, the Great Learning and the Doctrine of the Mean*; II, *The works of Mencius*, 2 vols. (Hongkong, 1861; rev. ed., Oxford, 1893-95).

[75] 儀禮. Cf. *supra*, this chapter, n. 69.

[76] The text adopted was that sponsored by 顏安樂 Yen An-lo, who founded a school within a school during the first century B.C. The work of Yen is now lost, as is that of 莊彭祖 Juang Peng-dzu, a rival contemporary interpreter of the Gung Yang tradition, who received appointment as Bo Shir from 宣帝 the Emperor Hsüan, 73-49 B.C., and for whose teaching a chair was created among 14 in the imperial college at 洛陽 Lo Yang in A.D. 29. Maspero, "La Composition," MCB, I, 166-167.

[77] For this Wei inscription the text was reproduced in three kinds of writing: the clerkly style, seal characters, and an archaistic script which was evidently intended to reproduce the archaic characters then already forgotten. Pelliot, "Les classiques gravés sur pierre sous les Wei en 240-248," TP, XXIII (1924), 1-4.

[78] Cf. *supra*, chap. II, n. 2.

In 317–322 a spurious "Canon of History" was presented to the Throne. It included not only the authentic twenty-nine chapters of 伏生 Fu Sheng and a forged version of Kung's additions, but also texts purporting to represent a preface and commentary by Kung, which may never have existed. Although this spurious text was accorded general acceptance, the medieval scholars exercised their ingenuity in attempting to restore the archaic form of individual characters. So much diversity was by this process introduced among current manuscripts, that the emperor in 744 commanded 衛包 Wei Bao to prepare a version entirely in modern script, which was declared alone authentic. All other manuscripts were to be deposited in the imperial archives, where in fact they disappeared completely until in the present century fragments were recovered from Dun Huang.[79]

The practice of cutting in stone had now definitely proved its worth, and the classics were again engraved between 836 and 841.[80] Naturally, the version of the

[79] Pelliot, "Le Chou King en caractères anciens," MAO, II, 135–158.

[80] The project was supervised by 鄭覃 Jeng Tan, 中國人名 大辭典 "Chinese Biographical Dictionary," p. 1568. The monumental style of writing was now abandoned for the modern, simpler, 楷書 kai shu, "model script." Chavannes has published clear photographs taken in 1907 from the tablets which are now in the 碑林 Bei Lin or "Forest of Stelae" at 西安 Si An. These include the "Changes," "Odes," and "History," Confucius' "Sayings," and the 爾雅 Er ya, a dictionary of glosses to ancient texts, compiled probably in the third century B.C. *Mission archéologique dans la Chine septentrionale, Planches* (Paris, 1909), pl. ccclvi-ccclxix (all but the last double). Not reproduced by him are the rituals, commentaries on the "Annals," and the 孝經 Hsiao jing or "Canon of Filial Piety." About 1928 also the notorious former governor of

"Canon of History" which was selected for perpetuation was Wei Bao's modern text of the spurious "ancient text." Mao's version of the "Odes" which Liu Hsin had championed had now finally displaced those of Lu, Han, and Tsi. That scholastic rivalry was no longer a motivating factor in this measure is shown by the fact that all three "Rituals" were published, together with all three commentaries on the "Spring and Autumn Annals."

Printing from wood blocks was itself given its first great impetus by government primarily as a means of authentication of the classic texts. Preservation of these from corruption was now regarded as a duty involving dynastic prestige. In 932 the short Later Tang dynasty undertook to print the first edition of the "Nine Classics" from blocks, basing the text avowedly upon that cut in stone a century before. Substitution of the cheaper material was dictated primarily by consideration of economy.

Even with adoption of block printing as a cheap means of preservation and authentication, the Chinese continued to put their trust in the superior durability of stone. Only six years after inception of the first wood-block edition, the contemporary western state of 蜀 Shu — precisely the one in which block printing

---

Shandung province 張宗昌 Jang Dzung-chang attempted to redeem his evil reputation by sponsoring a splendid wood-block edition in 74 large volumes, based upon inked squeezes taken from the tablets before damage in the great earthquake, which on Jan. 23, 1556, brought to 830,000 people death by drowning in floods released from the Yellow and Wei rivers. The standard 明史 "Ming History," XVIII, 7b8–9. This edition, entitled 唐開成石壁十二經 Tang Kai Cheng shir bi shir er jing, bears the imprint of the 葅忍堂 Bi Ren Tang.

had first been applied to secular literature — sponsored fresh engraving in stone, as did shortly afterward the great Sung dynasty. Eight centuries later the Manchu dynasty asserted its authority as defender of the purity of the "Thirteen Classics" by having them once more engraved upon tablets which were then set up in proximity to the National College and Confucian Temple at the capital.

CHAPTER IV

HISTORICAL CRITICISM

IN THE field of historical criticism[1] — the evaluation of individual statements contained in established texts — Chinese historians of the old school did not evolve those principles which are now regarded in East and West alike as an indispensable part of scientific historical method.

Traditional Chinese historical criticism aims always to attain categorical affirmation, whereas contemporary scholarship recognizes that history must often be content with a statement of probability. Diversity of critical method flows, in the last analysis, from this disparity of aim. Whereas Western scientific method accepts as proved only those facts which are attested by two or more independent sources[2] (with the exception of those which are of such obvious and indifferent character that misstatement is hardly possible), the traditional Chinese historian assumes that every documentary source is entitled to respect as a sincere attempt at truthful record, which presumably does not venture beyond reliable information. In accordance with this premise, every statement which is not contradicted is entitled to acceptance. In event of conflict, reconciliation is attempted;[3] or if this be impossible, an arbitrary

[1] Sometimes distinguished as internal or higher criticism.

[2] A statement found in only a single source can be reproduced only as such, with reference.

[3] A good example is given by Chavannes, *Mémoires historiques*, I, 299, n. 3.

choice is made between competing versions. Unfortunately, Chinese practice does not require reproduction of rejected alternatives,[4] nor even any indication that a choice has been made. Harmony of the facts is indeed demanded no less by Chinese than by Western historians, but the systems of dating based on reigns and the complex symbolism of the sexagenary cycle[5] which are employed in China have made detection of inconsistencies in chronology particularly difficult.[6]

Probably because of the seriousness which informs all historical writing in China, little attempt is made to consider the factor of sincerity. The criteria of possible advantage to the author or his group; of vanity on their behalf; of favorable or hostile bias in regard to men, doctrines, or institutions; of adherence to the forms demanded by precedent; of satisfaction to the reader; and of literary distortion; all are usually passed over. Yet they obviously require application.

Distortion of fact in official reports of military reverses was under the empire a simple necessity,

[4] But cf. *infra*, chap. VII, n. 31.

[5] These are discussed in the following chapter.

[6] It has been noted (*supra*, chap. III, n. 19) that Kang Yu-wei in 1891 accused Liu Hsin of forging or garbling the *Dzo juan* to please his patron Wang Mang. Not until 1932 did Maspero publish the demonstration based upon texts in the well-known standard *Han shu*, that Liu Hsin's work upon the *Dzo juan* was done fifteen or twenty years before the usurpation of Wang Mang. He shows further that Liu's demand for introduction of the *Dzo juan* into the official school was made only just prior to his own withdrawal from court between June 11 and November 22, 6 B.C., about a year after that of Wang Mang, whose return to power was then quite unpredictable and was in fact made possible only by the deaths of the empress and her grandson the young emperor in 2 and 1 B.C. "La Composition," MCB, I (1931–1932), 144–154.

because to confess failure was to court disgrace. Regard for the prestige of the imperial house is doubtless responsible for repetition in serious histories of the most improbable miracles of its members. Bias is often evident — in the obloquy which is heaped upon the First Emperor of the Tsin as an opponent of scholarship, and upon Wang Mang as a usurper, and in the contemptuous disregard of both Buddhists and Daoists by scholars in the Confucian tradition. Compliance with accustomed forms leads to many verbal inaccuracies; any action taken on direct behalf of the emperor, irrespective of his actual participation, is ordinarily reported as his own. In the case of books compiled under the auspices of an imperial commission, the titular heads of that commission are listed as the principal authors, no matter how nominal may have been their connection with its labors. Deference to the traditional majesty of the imperial ruling house dictates a systematically distorted presentation of relationships between the emperor or his agents and barbarian tribes, foreign powers, or domestic rebels. Conspicuous neglect of these proprieties is lèse-majesté, an offense almost sure to be reported to the throne, rendering the author liable to condign punishment. Most forms of literary distortion are rare in Chinese history, yet one deserves especial notice. Related events of several different days are often grouped together and reported under a single date in the imperial chronicles or other annals. The appearance of precise dating may mislead the unwary reader.

Among the criteria of accuracy some, such as the subjective causes of inaccurate observation and record —

hallucination, illusion, inexperience, stupidity, and prejudice — are in general totally disregarded. On the other hand, the Chinese have recognized the more common sources of error — poor situation, distraction, or inattention of the observer; confusion, delay, reliance on indirect information, or perfunctoriness, in preparation of his written report — and have attempted to eradicate them at their source. To this end elaborate provision was made by government for scrutiny of all imperial actions by competent observers under favorable conditions, and for prompt systematic registration of them.[7]

Chinese historians seldom expose themselves to the charge of recording matters beyond the scope of their documents and observations. Secret matters and personalia of all kinds that may be classed as dubious are relegated to the category of "old tales"[8] which enjoy hardly more repute as history than do the historical novels of the West. Facts affecting the empire as a whole or in large part, and gradual tendencies, find a place in the essays of the standard histories and in encyclopedic works, but are usually well supported by documentary data, or else stated with an extreme of caution.

It has been suggested that little attempt is usually made systematically to weigh probabilities. Certain factors of probability differ materially between China

---

[7] The prescriptions of the Manchu dynasty will be cited more in detail in the chapter on classification.

[8] 故事 *Gu shir*, or 野史 *yeh shir*, "unconventional histories." Collections of these are far more entertaining than sober history, but the author of them is not subject to the usual restraints of responsibility.

and Western lands. In the West deliberate misstatement is judged improbable in the case of facts which are widely known and easily verified. In China the same rule applies but is subject to an important practical qualification. Because all preferment and disgrace of superior officials under the old régime were dependent on the sole imperial will, it mattered little how widely known a fact might be if it were concealed from the emperor. Verification often involved quite serious difficulty, for officials would hesitate to incur enmity by giving unwelcome information concerning each other. Even in important matters the more vigorous and able emperors relied largely on direct observation. Inherent probability, too, is often disregarded, as it was in medieval Europe, perhaps for a similar reason — the lack of development of the natural sciences. After all, the gushing forth of a spring of water in a desert spot at the approach of an emperor, as a reflection of his virtue, is no more improbable than many a miracle long familiar to Western readers.

In summary it may be said that, whereas the traditional historians of China have endowed us with incomparably rich printed source materials of admirably tested authenticity and scrupulously established text, their conceptions of historical criticism differ at so many points from ours, that the scientific evaluation and integration of those sources remains a standing challenge to our own and to coming generations.

CHAPTER V

Synthesis

It has been seen that diversity of aim is in part responsible for important differences between Chinese and Western ideas of historical criticism. Quite equally fundamental divergencies differentiate Chinese and Western conceptions of historical writing itself. We in the West demand that an historian analyze and classify his facts for presentation in that logical sequence which shall seem to his individual brain best calculated to expose, not merely their order in time, but also the concatenation of cause and effect. We demand, moreover, that he create a faithful and lifelike reflection of past times, strange places, and unfamiliar personalities. The Chinese, on the contrary, conceive of the past as a series of concrete events and overt acts; and of history as a registration of them which should be exact and dispassionate, without any projection across the scene of the personality of the registrar, who must punctiliously refrain from garbling his presentation by his own perhaps imperfect appreciation of the true sequence of causation.

It is the function of the Chinese historian to collect the facts and to subject them to a process of discreet filtering which may only suppress those of insignificant importance and present those of greater moment to speak for themselves without interference. It is, of course, apparent that personality, however discreet, must be pitilessly reflected in the very choice of facts which are deemed worthy to be retained in the filter; but, as in all composition, the aim does condition the result, and a more or less complete anonymity in uniformity marks the product.

It follows from the Chinese conception of history as an impersonal record of events, that any historical account which may be written assumes a kind of independent existence, a corporate personality, divorced from any idea of proprietorship by its author. And accordingly, verbatim reproduction of the records of earlier historians, no matter how extensive, is to be regarded, not as plagiarism, but rather as the natural and reasonable process by which new histories of previously recorded events should be constructed. Historical writing ordinarily involves, not original composition of any considerable length, but compilation of choice selections from earlier works.

When a Pribram edits the "Secret Treaties of Austria-Hungary" or a MacMurray the "Treaties and Agreements with and concerning China," we do not expect the editors to paraphrase their documents. Indeed, were they to do so, we should limit our use of them to the requirements of necessity. Similarly, in the Chinese view, an historical account should not be committed to paper unless it be correct; and, if it be exact, any departure from its original phraseology — unless the literary form be unsatisfactory — should be scrupulously avoided.[1] Thus it happens that in the most

---

[1] The principle here enunciated evidently conflicts in spirit at least with the "praise and blame" concept mentioned on p. 13. It goes without saying that not all Chinese historians have realized their highest ideals.

unpretentious historical compilations of the old school
will be found imbedded exact transcripts from the
earliest known accounts of the events which they relate.

The method of compilation employed is essentially
primitive — synthesis of the simplest kind, accomplished by dissection of pre-existing works and arrangement of their component fragments in chronological
sequence.[2] Respect for the integrity of texts is so strong
in China that often no attempt is made to harmonize
the documents which are thus brought into juxtaposi-
tion. A classic illustration of this is afforded by the
"Commentary of Dzo," which reproduces documents
that are themselves compiled with reference to diverse
calendars in use among the feudal states of ancient
China, resulting in a confusion which no one has yet
been able to resolve.[3]

Chronological order is the accepted basis for nearly
all compilation. It may be strictly applied or may be
made subordinate to a topical plan. In either case,
recourse may be had to brief excursions into the past
or future, when such may become indispensable to
elementary comprehension. Subsidiary order, within
the limits of a single year or day, is often dictated by
prescriptions of traditional or ritual character.[4] Especially in the "basic annals" of the standard history

---

[2] Chavannes has identified the chief sources from which the
great work of Sz-ma Tsien is drawn: *Mémoires historiques*, I,
cxxiv-clxxi. An instructive example of his utilization of some of
these sources is presented by J. J. L. Duyvendak, *The Book of
Lord Shang* (London, 1928), pp. 35-39.

[3] Maspero, JA, CCXII (1928), 51, n. 2. For a brief account of
the "Commentary of Dzo" cf. *supra*, chap. II, n. 8.

[4] Cf. *infra*, pp. 89-90, 98.

form, it needs to be borne constantly in mind that dating is recorded with reference to the imperial court.[5]

Chinese dates are most often expressed with reference to imperial reigns. Contemporary events are cited as occurring in the first or second year of the current 年號 *nien hao* or (literally) "year name." The custom of assigning auspicious titles to each commencing reign period originated under the Emperor Wu of the Former Han dynasty, who ruled 140–87 B.C., and who assigned eleven distinctive titles to successive epochs of his long reign.[6] The third emperor of the Tang dynasty adopted no less than fourteen for the years A.D. 650–683. From the accession of the first emperor of the Ming in 1368, however, the tradition has become established that each emperor should select but a single "year name" for his whole reign. It is because of this innovation that, in speaking of the emperors of the last two dynasties, the *nien hao* is often cited as though it were a personal name. Kang Hsi ("Tranquil Peace"), for example, refers to the years 1662–1722, but is not, properly speaking, the name of the emperor, whose personal name is taboo to his subjects.[7] Writers may refer to an earlier emperor of their own or a preceding dynasty by his posthumous 廟號 *miao hao* or "temple

[5] Thus, e.g., in the "Annals" of the "Draft Tsing History," VI, 16b1–2, the death of the Grand Marshal 尚善 Shang-Shan is not recorded until Sept. 26, 1678, when it was reported to the emperor, although the report itself fixes the date of his demise on the previous May 23. 東華錄, *Dung Hua lu*, "Archival Records," XXII, 10a9–10.

[6] Pierre Hoang, "Prolégomènes à ia concordance néoménique," *Mélanges sur la chronologie chinoise* (*Variétés sinologiques*, no. 52 [Shanghai, 1920]), p. 134.

[7] The subject of taboos is discussed in some detail, *infra*, pp. 81–84.

name," the one which is inscribed upon his spirit-tablet enshrined in the Ancestral Temple. Thus the year 1663 may be optionally cited as 康熙二年 "the second year of Kang Hsi" or as 聖祖二年 "the second year of Sheng Dzu (the Holy Ancestor)." [8]

An alternative or supplementary system of dating refers to a cycle of sixty combinations of symbols which has been in use since a very early epoch to distinguish the sequence of days, and — at least since the Han period — of years also. [9] The elements of this sexagenary cycle are a series of ten, and another of twelve, rudimentary signs, which for purposes of illustration may be replaced by corresponding Arabic and Roman numerals. The sequence [10] of combination is as follows:

1 I,   2 II,   3 III, 4 IV, 5 V,   6 VI, 7 VII, 8 VIII, 9 IX, 10 X,
1 XI, 2 XII, 3 I,   4 II, 5 III, and so on.

When the denary series has been repeated six times and the duodenary series five times, with always different combinations, the sixtieth, 10 XII, is reached, and a new cycle is begun, as before, 1 I, 2 II, etc. As compared with our Western century the sexagenary cycle has three defects. Except to those who use them constantly, the combinations do not reveal immediately

---

[8] Cf. *infra*, pp. 81–82.

[9] Henri Havret and Chambeau ("Notes concernant la chronologie chinoise," *Mélanges sur la chronologie*, p. 2, n. 1) quote in this connection a passage from the 爾雅 *Er ya*, a glossary of the third century B.C., which, however, mentions only one of the sexagenary symbols at a time in connection with the movements of Jupiter, the "year-star."

[10]
甲子, 乙丑, 丙寅, 丁卯, 戊辰, 己巳, 庚午, 辛未, 壬申, 癸酉,
甲戌, 乙亥, 丙子, 丁丑, 戊寅, and so on.

their position within the cycle.[11] Because some of the
basic symbols are nearly alike in pronunciation, errors
in transcription are all too common. And finally, the
combinations carry no notation to indicate the particular cycle to which they refer.

Chinese writers of biography seldom trouble themselves about what we call vital statistics, the years of
birth and death of their subjects. All too frequently
independent biographies are found to be in categorical
conflict with regard to them. More significant in the
Chinese view are the dates of success in the official
examinations which are the normal high road to civil
service appointment. Record of conferment of the doctorate is particularly desirable, since that date ordinarily marks not only first appointment to office but also
the beginning of serious literary production. This date,
too, is easily checked from the records of the triennial
examinations.[12]

It is the practice of the "basic annals" in the standard
histories to cite each year with reference both to an
imperial reign and to the cycle in which it belongs. The
month is cited by number, and the day by cyclical
signs. With the aid of Pierre Hoang's admirable *Concordance des chronologies néoméniques chinoise et euro-*

[11] It should, however, be observed that the denary series corresponds directly with our decade and permits easy and immediate
equation to the final digit in any Christian date. E.g., the symbol
辛 *sin* always corresponds to a final 1 whether the date be A.D. 31,
641, or 1921; and 甲 *jia*, which opens the Chinese series, is in our
dates a final 4.

[12] Cf. e.g., 詞林輯略 *Sz lin dzi lüeh* by 朱汝珍 Ju Ru-jen,
11 chapters, 4 volumes, which lists chronologically all doctors 1646–
1904 with a supplementary volume of rhymed index.

péenne,[13] which indicates the cyclical signs for the first
day of each lunar month, and also the corresponding
day of the Western calendar, it is quite simple to con-
vert these dates to our own system of notation.

Certain features of modern historical writing are
conspicuously absent in the traditional product of
Chinese historians. Perhaps none is more sadly lacking
than bibliography and reference. Not only is no effort
whatever made to indicate the sources open to the
enquiring reader who would go further, or even, save in
exceptional cases, to substantiate with a list of titles
consulted the conclusions of the author; but individual
statements are ordinarily made ex cathedra without any
reference documentation. Long and arduous systematic research sometimes fails to reveal the source for
perfectly well-founded assertions. In those comparatively rare instances when previous books are cited, it
is considered adequate casually to mention the title or
author's surname, or at most to cite the chapter. The
resultant duplication of labor is obviously enormous. In
defense of traditional methods (or their lack) it is truly
said that editions differ widely in bulk, so that a page
reference which is exact for one is not so for another.
At the same time, it is undeniable that there is serious
advantage in knowing whether a passage occurs, within
the separately paged chapter, on folio 1 or folio 20 in an
author's copy, even though the edition may remain unknown. It is plain also that identification of editions
used and to which reference is made, is highly de-

---

[13] *Variétés sinologiques*, no. 29 (Shanghai, 1910). There are also
Chinese manuals, some of which supply concordance with Western
dating.

sirable. Indeed, given the slowness of reading Chinese texts which hampers even the best sinologists, there is often positive gain in making reference, not merely to the folio, but to the page and line. Such precise reference is valuable, if only to the original author.

An almost equally conspicuous omission in the Chinese scheme of history is the background of events. With all too rare exceptions we are left to rely wholly on imagination for the personality and appearance of even the leading actors. What we should call an intimate picture is really never drawn. Nor are we better off in the matter of material setting, for no word of description is vouchsafed in connection with narrative. If we turn to the "Illustrations" which accompany the "Collected Institutes" of the Manchu dynasty we find indeed punctiliously exact representations of the places of imperial worship, together with their precise specifications. But these are supplied for ritual reasons, and neither pictures nor texts describe even the palaces for secular residence.[14]

Private life of any kind lies outside the domain of the traditional historian. The emperor, as a model of filial piety to his empire, performs a public duty by honoring the elders of his family. Thus the "Basic Annals"[15] of the "Draft Tsing History" record how, in 1678, the emperor escorted the grand dowager-empress to the Hot Springs. They mention also in the same year the birth of a son who was to become his

[14] Exception should be made for certain illustrations which commemorate imperial festivals of longevity, progresses, or victories. Pelliot, "Les Conquêtes de l'Empereur," TP, XX (1921), 183–274.
[15] VI, 16b7.

father's successor. But they ignore a merely private grief, the consequent death of the boy's mother, a favorite concubine, although it led the emperor to wear mourning for five days, to confer a posthumous title upon her, and to write a lengthy composition expressing his feelings.[16]

Causation, as already suggested, is seldom indicated directly. This is the more to be regretted because the springs of action in China often differ radically from those which are familiar in Western history. They depend of necessity upon a variety of factors — education, morals, economics, governmental and social organization — which are not easily reconstructed in their entirety. We are often reduced to guess almost blindly at what must have been, in the time of a competent but silent historian, matters of common knowledge.

Gradual change also is hardly recorded by the Chinese historian. It does not readily accommodate itself to the hand of the chronicler, for no date can be assigned to it. Seldom does it admit of precise or quantitative statement. It finds a place, indeed, in the essays of the standard history form, but even there it tends to be neglected unless by chance it be thrown into relief by recognition in a memorial or imperial edict.

One final omission is borne in upon the reader of Chinese history — an omission which by implication was noted at the outset. He closes his book without having established any serious contact with its author. Gone are the systematic presentation of facts, the illuminating textual and footnote commentary upon

---

[16] "Draft Tsing History," "Biographies," I, 8a9–9a4.

them, the judicious summary — all those elements of personal guidance which we are wont to expect from a specialist who writes upon his own subject. We are left instead in the hard, cold world to analyze our facts as best we can and to struggle with our feeble light to appraise and to interpret.

CHAPTER VI

STYLE

IT APPEARS that already at a very early period Chinese writers became conscious of literary style and made a definite effort to adapt it to various kinds of composition, demarcating clearly the distinction between documents, annals, and romances, as well as that between philosophy and poetry. Thus Maspero believes [1] that the texts which have been united in the authentic portion of the "Canon of History" [2] were composed by diverse writers; and that their stylistic uniformity springs, not only from general similarity of date (ninth to sixth centuries B.C.), but from a common conscious effort.

Whatever may be the truth of this interpretation, certain it is that the "Commentary of Dzo," [3] which was compiled about 300 B.C., presents a series of diverse documents that have been reduced to pronounced stylistic uniformity. The same uniformity and an equal degree of anonymity are exhibited in the "Historical

---

[1] Review, JA, CCXII (1928), 159–165 (esp. 161, n. 1, 164–165), of Karlgren's Tso chuan, GHÅ, XXXII, no. 3 (1926). Karlgren had proposed to see in the diverse styles of early documents variety of territorial origin, a view which he defends in his Ancient Texts, BMFEA, I (1929), 165–183, esp. 177–183. Maspero, however, reiterates his own conclusion in a fresh review, JA, CCXXII (1933), "Bulletin critique," pp. 38–48, esp. 45–48.

[2] Cf. *supra*, p. 8, n. 2, and p. 61.

[3] Cf. *supra*, chap. II, n. 8.

Memoirs" of Sz-ma Tan and Sz-ma Tsien.[4]   Indeed,
the literary style of this first and greatest of the standard histories is so remarkably impersonal that even
Chavannes, its translator, concludes that it is impossible to determine, even among passages dealing with
the time of the authors themselves, which are original
composition and which are mere reproduction of the
work of others.[5]

The literary style of the "Commentary of Dzo"
belongs to the fourth century B.C., and that of the
"Historical Memoirs" to the first. Just as the two are
unlike, so do the styles of later imitators differ. It is
not, however, the points of difference, but those of
similarity which must here concern us.

Historical composition in Chinese has evolved a
considerable body of conventional diction which
requires special study for complete comprehension. In
this respect it is not unlike other branches of Chinese
literature, for each has found it expedient to create a
distinctive vocabulary. In the case of history it does
not spring from selfish desire to cloak esoteric ideas in
obscurity, nor from pedantic insistence upon forced
purism, though both these motives appear in some other
types of literature. A good quality of expression is
indeed expected, but any forced striving after literary
effect is exceptional. Rather on the contrary, uniformity
of subject matter leads logically to uniformity of expres-

[4] Cf. *supra*, pp. 16–17. Naturally their citation of such documents as the "Canon of History" and the "Commentary of Dzo,"
which were already centuries old, results in contrast of style.

[5] *Mémoires historiques*, I, lxi. This observation does not, of
course, apply to the brief critical notes appended by Sz-ma to his
biographies.

sion; variety of phraseology is neither expected nor desired.

The rather numerous conventions which govern reference to the reigning dynasty and its members are of necessity of universal application. Indeed, a thorough knowledge of this subject was a prerequisite to success at the civil service examinations; failure to observe the official prescriptions might even entail summary physical punishment.

The subjects of any dynasty seldom refer to it by name, ordinarily preferring to distinguish it by some one of the circumlocutions: 皇朝 *Huang Chao*, 國朝 *Guo Chao*, 我朝 *Wo Chao*, or 大朝 *Da Chao*, the "Imperial," "National," "Our," or simply the "Great Dynasty." The dynastic name may at need be invoked, but should be accompanied by suitable testimonial of respect. This may be, and often is, indicated by breaking the line of text at its occurrence so that the name may stand at the top of a fresh column of characters, perhaps even above the ordinary upper textual margin, or at least be preceded by a blank.

Mention of the imperial ancestors is accomplished by use of the 廟號 *miao hao* or "temple name," with or without addition of the distinctive final element in the 尊諡 *dzun shir* or honorific posthumous title.[6] In either case, demonstration of special respect is incumbent. In mentioning the emperors of earlier dynasties, the honorific is omitted, since its inclusion would imply a sentiment of loyalty unfavorable to the reigning house;

---

[6] Cf. *supra*, pp. 72–73. A dozen or so laudatory epithets were engraved on jade plaques and stored in the Ancestral Temple, but this one alone was inscribed on the emperor's spirit-tablet after his temple name and was shared with each of his empresses.

and, since many of the "temple names" recur repeatedly in history, the name of the dynasty is prefixed.
The latter is less often coupled with the posthumous
title. So it happens that the emperor who from 1723
to 1912 was known as 國朝聖祖仁皇帝 Guo Chao Sheng
Dzu Ren Huang Di, or "The National Dynasty's Holy
Ancestor, the Benevolent Emperor," has become simply
清聖祖 Tsing Sheng Dzu or Tsing Ren Di. Very often
the mention of any imperial name is avoided by reference to a 年燁 *nien hao* or reign period — such as 康熙
Kang Hsi — either past or present.

Most rigorous of the prescriptions that surround the
imperial appellations are those which render taboo any
reference to the personal name of an emperor of the
reigning dynasty. Because the use of personal names
implies a commanding degree of familiarity, it is
restricted in all cases to elders and superiors throughout Chinese society. It will then be readily understood
that mention of the 御名 *yü ming* or imperial name involves an arrogation of superiority to the emperor himself. There results the curious paradox that, while the
proper name of an emperor might never appear in print,
every literate subject of his dynasty was required to
know and to remember it solely that he might avoid it.

The taboo of personal names leads to a variety of
literary expedients. If, in quoting a specific text, a
taboo character be encountered, it may be transcribed
with omission of one or more conspicuous strokes. Thus
in the 康熙字典 *Kang Hsi Dz Dien*, "Dictionary of the
Kang Hsi Period," [7] which is obviously the highest

[7] Palace edition, 40 volumes (1710–1716), 午集上, 1a, and 巳
集中, 39a.

authority on the question, the personal name of the reigning Emperor, which is properly 玄燁 Hsüan-yeh,[8] is honored by conspicuous designation, but is atrophied by omission of the final stroke of each character, so as to appear 玄燁.[9] Even this deformation was held to approach too nearly the sacred name. Another character of generally similar form or sound is sometimes substituted, and so it was in this case. The common character 元 *yüan* is designated to take the place of 玄 *hsüan*, and all examination candidates during the later reigns of the dynasty were required to effect the substitution.[10] Sometimes no character at all is substituted,

---

[8] It signifies "Flash of Fire in Darkness," but the meaning is of slight importance. Each son in a generation is assigned as the first element in his personal name the same character from a passage in literature which has been selected as auspicious for the family. The sons of the next generation are named with the following character, and so on until the passage is finished, when a new one will be chosen. By this means the Chinese greatly simplify the study of genealogy, and the keeping of records which are essential to ancestral sacrifice.

The second element of the name is indicated by earlier dictionaries to be a mere graphic variant of 燁. But the *Kang Hsi dz dien* records the latter in a separate citation, 巳集中, 50b5, with no other distinction than tacit omission of the final stroke.

[9] 玄 came to be regarded as almost equivalent to 玄. The former appears by error in the first sentence of the "Basic Annals," chap. VI of the "Draft Tsing History," which is set from type.

[10] *Hsüan*, which means "dark," "mysterious," is constantly used in Daoist texts. Substitution of *yüan*, which commonly appears also with its own proper meaning of "first," "original," resulted in much confusion until reprint, after the revolution, of a Ming edition of the Daoist canon. Dr. J. R. Ware has called attention to similar confusion in writing the name of the famous Tang Buddhist pilgrim 玄奘 Hsüan-dzang, in which the same substitution of 元 has led to widespread misconception. "Transliteration of the Names of Chinese Buddhist monks," *Journal of the American Oriental Society*, LII (1932), 159–162, n. 5.

but in its place is inserted a hollow square.[11] So complete and constant was the taboo of imperial names, and so rigorous its enforcement, that a subject hardly dared even to pronounce one. Indeed, certain harmless written expressions were forbidden because their oral pronunciation sounded like disloyal utterances. It is doubtless to overcome such hesitancy that the emperor in 1685 took occasion to ordain by edict that during prayers in the Ancestral Temple, in order to manifest proper respect for his forebears, his name should be read out loud and clear.[12]

Direct mention of the reigning emperor is permitted to his subjects only through the general titles 帝 *Di*, "Emperor," 皇上 *Huang Shang*, "Imperial One Above," or simply *Shang*, "Superior One." Usually any direct reference is avoided by employment of a series of special terms which signify imperial action: 詔 *jao*, "to decree"; 諭 *yü*, "to speak or issue an edict"; 旨 *jir*, "to issue a rescript or express the imperial will";

---

[11] Cf. also Aurousseau's filled square: BEFEO, XII, no. 9 (1912), 68.

[12] "Basic Annals," VII, 4b13–15a1. It should be added that, from similar motives of respect, the personal names of Confucius and Mencius are traditionally taboo.

An excellent general study of taboo names throughout history is entitled 史諱舉例 *Shir wei jü li* by 陳垣 Chen Yüan, 燕京學報 *Yenching Journal*, IV (December 1928), 537–651. For the Tsing period it is less detailed than that of Arnold Vissière, which is especially devoted to it: "Traité des caractères chinois que l'on évite par respect," JA, 9e sér., XVIII (1901), 320–373. It is regrettable that Erich Haenisch had no opportunity to consult Chen's work in preparing his article, "Die Heiligung des Vater- und Fürstennamens in China, ihre ethische Begründung und ihre Bedeutung in Leben und Schrifttum," *Verhandlungen der Sächsischen Akademie der Wissenschaften*, LXXXIV, no. 4 (Leipzig, 1932), 1–20.

御 *yü*, "to prescribe or direct," "to go to or be present in"; 幸 *hsing*, "to make a progress"; 賜 *sz*, "to bestow or confer"; 膳 *shan*, "to eat"; and 崩 *beng*, "to die." Complementary to these expressions there is a second series which denotes action towards or on behalf of the emperor: 上 *shang*, "to offer up"; 奏 *dzou*, "to present a memorial," etc.

Not only imperial nomenclature and personal actions, but all kinds of other matters have been codified into conventional stylistic formulae. All of the regular processes of administration are recorded with compactness. Two complete parallel sets of terms differentiate the movements, success, or failure of the imperial and rebel arms respectively. Particularly laconic are the expressions which indicate ritual, and the ominous manifestations of nature. Truly it may be said of the style of Chinese history, as of the intricate conventions of Chinese social intercourse, that it reflects the accumulated usages of the world's most hoary unbroken tradition.

CHAPTER VII

FORMAL CLASSIFICATION

CLASSIFICATION is in Western countries regarded as
the exclusive concern of the librarian. In China, however, it is a constant preoccupation of the historian.
Not only bibliographic research (*Heuristik*), but the writing of history itself, are vitally affected by largely formal
distinctions which have been canonized by custom.

Already in the time of Christ the "Seven Summaries" of Liu Hsin [1] segregated as "classics" all those
texts which were then supposed to have some connection with Confucius. By the seventh century the
scheme of classification appears in practically its
modern pattern in the "Essay on Literature" of the
"Sui History." [2] Already it is dominated by a fourfold
division: classics, history, philosophy, and letters. In
the first group are included such historical texts as the
"Canon of History" and the "Commentary of Dzo." [3]
Within the third are found scientific and legal works,
histories of painting, and encyclopedias. Among the
collected works of literary men are also the works of
historians and statesmen. In the main, however, the
vast bulk of literature of definitely historical character is placed in the category "history," and is there
now subdivided into fifteen classes, some of which are

[1] Cf. *supra*, pp. 33–35.
[2] Cf. *supra*, p. 8.
[3] Cf. *supra*, pp. 8 and 61; and 11, n. 8, respectively.

determined by content, and others by the method of composition.

Foremost among them all come the 正史 *Jeng Shir*, or "Standard Histories," which with their various comprehensive and special commentaries stand naturally apart as the source from which many of the others have been quarried. The first, the "Historical Memoirs," [4] is a comprehensive history of the Chinese people from the lengendary epoch down to the time of the compilers in the reign of 漢武帝 the Emperor Wu of the Han, 140–87 B.C. The second, the "History of the Former Han," [5] which was compiled in the first century A.D., follows faithfully in most respects the precedents already established, but creates a new one through restriction to the period of a single dynasty which had already fallen. When in later centuries new standard histories were compiled, they took always as their model these earliest and greatest of their class. Together they form a continuous series covering the whole of recorded history from the beginning to 1912. Because, with few exceptions, each is confined to a single dynasty, they are often called by Western writers the "dynastic histories."

The distinguishing characteristic of all these works is division into mutually complementary parts which are clearly defined by precedent, which are divergent in subject and method, and each of which treats comprehensively the entire period. The first place is occupied by a concise chronicle of the court and of major events in the empire, arranged chronologically and

[4] Cf. *supra*, pp. 16–17.
[5] Cf. *supra*, pp. 32, n. 35, and 35–36.

precisely dated. A second part comprises essays, eight to sixteen in number, into which is compressed much information concerning the principal problems of government. The third section usually included consists in tables which set forth the genealogy of the imperial family and the succession of ministers of state. The fourth part, which usually occupies over half the work, consists in biographies of prominent personages who are grouped according to their careers.

It must be admitted that at least the later standard histories have a valid claim on grounds of authenticity as well as form to recognition as standard. Their peculiarly authentic character is derived from the official manuscript sources upon which they are based.

Traditional primary sources for the basic annals are the 起居注 *Chi Jü Ju* or "Diaries of Activity and Repose," which record in minute detail all the public doings and sayings of each emperor, together with all business, governmental or other, in which he shared. The practice of compiling these diaries dates from the time of 漢明帝 the Emperor Ming (A.D. 58–75) of the Han; [6] but, doubtless because of their bulk, the diaries of the earlier dynasties have completely disappeared.

---

[6] 漢唐宋起居注考 *Han Tang Sung chi jü ju kao*, "Investigation of the Imperial Diaries of the Han, Tang, and Sung," by 朱希祖 Ju Hsi-dzu, 國學季刊 *Guo hsüeh ji kan*, "Journal of Sinological Studies" of the Peking National University, II, no. 4 (December 1930), 629–640. The 隋書經籍志 "Essay on Literature" in the standard "Sui History," XXXIII, 10b–11a3, traces the history of the diaries back to the Jou dynasty, when it was already customary to record the orders of the king. It errs however in repeating the mention by the 西京雜記 *Si Jing dza ji*, "Miscellaneous Records of the Western Capital," of a diary of the Emperor Wu (140–87 B.C.) in one roll, which is said in the preface

The "Collected Institutes" of the Manchu dynasty [7] fortunately contain the detailed prescriptions which governed preparation of the "Diaries" during that epoch. In 1670, the ninth year of the Kang Hsi period, the emperor created a special bureau, the 起居注館 Chi Jü Ju Guan, composed of ten Manchus and twelve Chinese from the Academy of Letters and Supervisorate of Instruction,[8] to be responsible for their compilation. Thereafter until the fall of the dynasty, no significant public act of an emperor was performed without the presence of its representatives. During transaction of government business no less than four officials were required to stand close by as auditors and eyewitnesses, and the prescription is formal that upon withdrawal they should prepare their notes immediately.

The sequence of record is stipulated: first must come edicts; then state papers prepared in the ministries, and those transmitted through them; then memorials from the Manchu Eight Banners, and from officials of the capital and the provinces, public matters before private; then interviews with representatives of the various ministries and bureaus, and finally, of the Banners. In recording the edicts, the order of importance must be followed, matters concerning the altars, temples, or tombs placed first. Ministerial papers must be cited

---

of that work to have been in the possession of 葛洪 Go Hung of the fourth century. Not only is no such work recorded in the inventories of Liu Hsiang and Liu Hsin, as Ju Hsi-dzu points out, but the *Si Jing dza ji* is itself a forgery, apparently of the sixth-century writer 吳均 Wu Jün. Cf. Pelliot, TP, XXVII (1930), 389.

[7] 大清會典 *Da Tsing hui dien*, LXX, 9a–12b (ed. 1899).

[8] 翰林院 Han Lin Yüan and 詹事府 Jan Shir Fu, respectively.

according to the precedence of their sources: the Grand
Secretariat, the Imperial Clan Court, the Academy of
Letters, the six Ministries of Public Office, Finance,
Ceremonial, War, Justice, and Public Works, the Cen-
sorate, and the Bureau of Mongolian Affairs. If it hap-
pened there were any memorial from the Ministry of Ceremonial concerning the presentation of congratulations
or from the Court of Ceremonial Worship [9] regarding
the sacrifices, these should be placed before the business
of the Grand Secretariat. The order of precedence for
other items of record was no less minutely determined.

Two volumes of these "Diaries" were designated
for every month; but in accordance with precedent
the twenty-four for each year were compiled only in
the following year. The preliminary manuscripts first
prepared were revised in detail and additions or alterations made by the Director of the Bureau of Record,
then sent to the Director of the Academy of Letters to
be read and passed upon. They were then dated exactly
and inscribed with the names of the officials responsible
for them. After they had been provided with prefaces
and closing remarks, they were sealed up with the seal
of the Academy of Letters and deposited in gilded metal
coffers which were in turn locked and sealed. Finally,
in the twelfth month of each year, a report to the
Emperor was prepared, the "Diaries" were sent to the
Grand Secretariat, and their compilers, together with
the Under-Secretaries, supervised their deposition in
all the repositories.[10]

[9] 太常寺 Tai Chang Sz.
[10] This last phrase, 諸庫 ju ku, is rather enigmatic, since actually
the "Diaries" in definitive form have been reported found only in
the Archives of the Grand Secretariat. Apparently all other logical

The first work traditionally to be based upon the "Diaries" is the 實錄 *Shir Lu,* "Veritable Record," of each emperor, which is compiled at the close of his reign by the filial care of his successor. With few exceptions the "Veritable Records" of early dynasties have disappeared; but those of the Ming have been preserved, partly in the Wade collection of the University of Cambridge,[11] partly in the National Library of Beiping.[12]

---

places of deposit in Peking have been searched. May another copy exist at Mukden? The copy which was originally stored in the ground floor of the Archives is in two sets, Manchu and Chinese. The latter covers the period 1671-1908 in 4,558 volumes, but with the exception of the Hsien Feng era (1851-1861) no part is complete. It was transferred in March 1931 to the 大高殿 Da Gao Dien, or Imperial Rain Temple, for inventory; but the Manchu version in 4,679 volumes was left in the Archives. The original Chinese drafts for the Diaries were sent to the 國史館 Guo Shir Guan, or "Bureau of National History," as soon as the definitive compilations were accepted, but the set actually found there and transferred in November 1929 to the 南三所 Nan San So, the offices of the Archival Division of the Palace Museum, extends only from 1723-1909 (omitting the Kang Hsi period entirely) in only 2,597 volumes. 北平故宮博物院文獻館一覽, "Survey of the Archival Division of the Beiping Palace Museum" (1932), esp. folios 4a5, 4b2, 12b5-13. All three versions of the "Diaries" were sent to Shanghai in the spring of 1932 to avoid danger of seizure by the Japanese. 故宮博物院文獻館二十二年度工作報告及將來計畫 "Report of the Work of the Archival Division of the Beiping Palace Museum for 1933 and Its Future Plans" (1934), esp. folios 2a9-12.

[11] H. A. Giles, *Catalogue of the Wade collection of Chinese and Manchu Books in the Library of the University of Cambridge* (Cambridge, 1898), pp. 76-78, nos. B1870-1954.

[12] Aurousseau (BEFEO, XII, no. 9 [1912], 72-75) presents a lucid inventory of these last, and also notes on the earlier works of this class which have survived. Walter Fuchs states that three old sets of private copies exist in Tōkyō and a fourth in Seoul. "The Personal Chronicle of the First Manchu Emperor," *Pacific Affairs,* IX (1936), 78-85, esp. 83.

The Tsing dynasty in its turn was not slow to follow imperial precedent. Preparation of the "Veritable Record" of the founder of the dynasty was begun in 1636,[13] the very year when its imperial pretensions were proclaimed at Mukden. During the Kang Hsi period this same work was revised between 1682 and 1686; [14] the record of the second emperor was ordered examined in 1667 and revised six years later; while the record of the first emperor to rule at Peking was begun in 1667 and completed five years later.[15] The 聖祖仁皇帝實錄 or "Veritable Record of the Holy Ancestor and Benevolent Emperor" [16] was in turn begun in the final month

---

[13] The most authentic sources for dating these imperial editions are the 國朝宮史 *Guo chao gung shir*, "History of the Palace under the Present Dynasty," which was compiled in manuscript by imperial commission, 1761–1769, and published by 羅振玉 Lo Jen-yü (1925), 36 chapters, 10 volumes, esp. XXII, 2a–5a; and the 故宮殿本書庫現存目 *Gu Gung Dien Ben Shu Ku hsien tsun mu*, "Catalogue of Works Now Preserved in the Palace Library of Imperial Editions" (1933), 3 chapters, 3 volumes, I, 2b–3a.

[14] This latter date is supplied by the "Draft Tsing History," "Basic Annals," VII, 6a9.

[15] All of these three works were provided with prefaces in 1734; but in the Chien Lung era they were subjected to a new revision which was completed in 1739. This latest revision seems to have entailed many changes of fact and in transcription of proper names from Manchu to Chinese. This fact is noted by 稻葉岩吉 (君山) Inaba Iwakichi (Kunzan) in his 清朝全史 *Tsing chao tsüan shir* (Chinese translation, 1914), II, 62–64, following a Japanese edition of the original version, which appeared in 1807. It is confirmed by the recent 1933 "Report of the Archival Division of the Palace Museum," 5b1–6. Much further information concerning these earlier works is given by Fuchs in a notable chapter, "Uber die Shihlu der Mandju-dynastie" (pp. 58–71) in his *Beiträge zur Mandjurischen Bibliographie und Literatur* (Tōkyō, 1936). I am indebted to Professor Knight Biggerstaff for calling my attention to this work.

[16] For this temple name and posthumous title, cf. *supra*, pp. 73 and 81–82.

of the closing year of the Kang Hsi era (1722), only a month after the decease of its subject, and actually two months before presentation of his posthumous title. Thereafter this precedent was followed regularly, each "Veritable Record" being prepared immediately after the demise of the emperor whose public life was thus recorded.

During the Tsing period five series of manuscript copies of each record were prepared by a special bureau created for the purpose. Each of these five series comprises sets in the Chinese, Manchu, and Mongol languages, save that for the Guang Hsü period (1875–1908) there is one only, in Chinese.[17]

---

[17] A series in large format bound in red damask was deposited within the precincts of the imperial palace at Mukden. This series, unlike the others, lacks the Mongol set. The government of Manchoukuo in 1936 printed the Chinese edition for publication. A second series in large format, bound in red damask, was deposited in Peking in the Imperial Historical Archives building, 皇史崴 Huang Shir Cheng, a windowless stone structure situated southeast of the Forbidden City.   Built by a Ming emperor in 1534, it was used by both Ming and Manchu dynasties for the safekeeping of the "Veritable Records" and "Sacred Precepts" (state papers of each reign edited by the succeeding emperor for immediate publication).   These documents are encased in gilded coffers which stand in rows upon a marble terrace within the building, safe from dampness, fire, and theft.   In June 1930 an inventory showed that the Chinese set of the *Shir lu*, covering the period 1616–1908, extends to 3,619 volumes and lacks 246.   The Manchu and Mongol sets, which end in 1874, each comprise 3,747 volumes and lack but 44.

A smaller series, also bound in red, was deposited in the buildings which flank the 乾清宮 Chien Tsing Gung, a central reception hall of the Forbidden City. According to an inventory in 1930, the three sets of this series lack but 9, 52, and 16 volumes respectively of the 3,791 which should cover the period 1616–1874. Consequently, the Chinese set of this series appears to be the most nearly complete in China.

Two further copies, bound respectively in red and yellow, were deposited in the Archives of the Grand Secretariat. The Chinese

Much as the "Basic Annals" of the standard histories derive their authority from the "Diaries" and "Veritable Records" upon which they are largely based, so the other divisions of the standard histories likewise are founded in part upon special manuscript compilations.

An important constituent of the government archives was the 紅本 *Hung Ben*, or "Red Copies" of all imperial decisions on administrative matters. Their name is derived from the fact that such documents were bound in red after having been passed upon by the Grand Secretariat and having received expression of the imperial will (奉旨 feng jir). Based directly upon them are the still voluminous 史書 *Shir Shu*, or "Historical Digests," of which each of the six Ministries of Civil

and Manchu sets from the complete series bound in red were sent in 1930 to the government offices in Nanking. The yellow Chinese set has been moved to the Imperial Rain Temple, while the yellow set in Manchu and the two in Mongol remain as before in the Archives. This Chinese set lacks 119 volumes, that in Manchu 12 volumes, and the two in Mongol 12 and 5, respectively.

In addition to the five series which have just been mentioned, two considerable sets of Chinese drafts have been found among the papers of the Bureau of Tsing History, but unfortunately both of them are in fragmentary condition. One set, in rectangular format, contains 3,297 volumes covering the period 1616–1908; the second, which stops with 1874, contains only 1,530 volumes. There are, in addition, 46 other volumes which have been copied by the Bureau from recognized sets. The draft sets are of special interest because they include the original version of the three earliest records, prior to the revision of 1739. Most of the information which has here been presented is drawn from the "Survey of the Archival Division of the Beiping Palace Museum," already cited, 10b–11b13. About 150 套 *tao* or cloth cases containing a large red-bound set of the Chinese *Shir lu* for the last half of the Kang Hsi era, 1691–1722, and the first half of the Guang Hsü period, 1875–1895, have been recently acquired by a Japanese library.

Office, Finance, Ceremonial, War, Justice, and Public
Works prepared a monthly volume.[18] These "Digests"
in turn provide invaluable documentation for the
"Essays" of the standard history. Similarly important
sources for the "Tables" are the 玉牒 *Yü Dieh*, or
"Jade Registers," which contain the separate genealogies of the Imperial Clan and its Collateral Kins-
men. These were subjected to official revision by the
Clan Court every decade.[19] For biography, besides the

[18] Of these the Archival Section of the Palace Museum alone now
has custody of more than 24,000 volumes shelved on 29 stack units,
while of the "Red Copies," upon which they are based, it has 3,500
bundles which require 101 stack units. "Survey," 8b–9a. On p. 8a
it retraces briefly the checkered fortunes of other extensive portions
of the documents from the archives of the Grand Secretariat, some
of which ultimately passed to the Historical Museum, and others
to the Sinological Research Institute of the Peking National University, while still others were destroyed by a paper merchant. This
story has been translated from an account by Lo Jen-yü by Pelliot,
TP, XX (1921), 243, n. The later history of the documents is given
by A. K. Chiu, "Chinese Historical Documents of the Ch'ing
Dynasty, 1644–1911," *Pacific Historical Review* (September 1932),
pp. 324–336, esp. 325–326; and C. H. Peake, "Documents Available
for Research on the Modern History of China," *American Historical Review*, XXXVIII, no. 1 (October 1932), 61–70, esp. 62–63. It
is presented in more detail by 徐中舒 Sü Jung-shu in his 內閣檔
案之由來及其整理, "Origin of the Grand Secretariat Documents
and Their Inventory" (14 folios, 1 plate), in 明清史料 *Ming
Tsing shir liao*, "Historical Materials of the Ming and Tsing Dynasties" (1930), vol. I. The series of "Red Copies" here cited begins
only with the Chien Lung period. Possibly earlier portions exist
elsewhere. Thanks to an inventory of the papers in possession of
the Bureau of Tsing History, we know that it had made selective
copies of the "Digests" to the number of 310 volumes. "Survey,"
9a12–10b3.

[19] Many of these have come to light in the Chien Tsing Gung,
the 壽皇殿 Shou Huang Dien or Imperial Hall of Longevity, and
the Imperial Clan Court.

well-known voluminous printed sources, both official
and private, the Bureau of National Historiography
compiled an extensive manuscript 國史大臣功臣列傳
Guo Shir Da Chen Gung Chen Lieh Juan, "Biographies
of Great and Meritorious Ministers of the Reigning
Dynasty." [20]

It is a curious evidence of the recognition by Chinese
and alien emperors alike of the temporary nature of
their dynastic tenure that, while the sovereigns of the
Ming and Tsing took pains to publish standard histories of the dynasties they had overthrown and to
prepare the extensive materials just described, they
never published these latter or contemplated immediate
preparation of standard histories of their own dynasties
to supplement the accepted series.[21] It has long been

[20] Of this work the Gest Oriental Library of the Institute for
Advanced Study at Princeton possesses 175 volumes, and another
copy in a Japanese library extends to 192 volumes covering the
period from the beginning of the dynasty to the middle of the Chien
Lung period (1736–1795). I am indebted to Dr. C. H. Peake for
this information. Dr. Knight Biggerstaff, who has had opportunity
to compare certain specimen biographies of the Beiping manuscript
with the printed repertories, has found them identical.

[21] Each dynasty vaunted its own permanence, and each emperor
was showered with wishes of life eternal, yet all recognized the truth
which was bluntly stated by 劉向 Liu Hsiang (79–8 B.C.) in a memorial presented after 32 B.C. ("History of the Former Han," XXXVI,
22b7–9): "Though one may have the saintliness of Yao and Shun
[rulers of the legendary golden age], he cannot alter a son like Dan
Ju [debased son of the former, who was accordingly excluded from
succession]. Though he may have the virtue of Yü and Tang [ideal-
ized founders of the Hsia and Shang], he cannot admonish his last
descendant like Jieh and Jou [degenerate last kings of those dynas-
ties]. From antiquity until now there has been no empire which
did not meet its end." For details concerning the persons mentioned cf. Chavannes, *Mémoires historiques*, vol. I, Index 1.

established custom that the standard history of each dynasty may be compiled only by its successor.

Several of the earlier standard histories were the work of individuals, but most of the more recent ones have been compiled by commissions: the "Ming History," for example, required almost forty-six years of labor, despite both a corps of fifty-three [22] scholars appointed at its inception in 1679 and the active interest of the emperor. Twenty-four of these histories were recognized as standard by inclusion in an imperial reprint in 1739; and the 新元史 *Sin Yüan Shir*, "New Yüan History," by a single scholar, 柯劭忞 Ko Shao-min, has since the republic been recognized by the government as worthy to rank as the twenty-fifth.

One of the first tasks undertaken by the republican government upon its establishment in 1912 was the preparation of the official history of the fallen dynasty, an enterprise which placed a visible seal of finality on the termination of Manchu rule in China. Compilation of this last standard history required the efforts of some sixty scholars through a period of fourteen years from its inception in 1914 until hurried publication in 1927–28. Although the Nationalist Government has refused recognition to the *Tsing Shir Gao*, or "Draft Tsing History," and has announced its intention to

---

[22] The "Draft of the Tsing History" (VI, 17a9–10) mentions the appointment of fifty workers besides three directors. Wylie (*Notes*, p. 24), speaks of fifty-eight. In 1687 the emperor urged the commission to base its labors upon the "Veritable Records" of the Ming. "Draft Tsing History," VII, 7b9–10. 明史編纂攷略 "Brief Study of the Compilation of the 'Ming History'" by 黃雲眉 Huang Yün-mei in the 金陵學報 *Nanking Journal*, I, no. 2 (November 1931), 323–360.

revise certain passages which are deemed reactionary, the work remains a typical and fairly creditable specimen of its class.[23]

Like other modern "standard histories," this one is divided into four parts. The 本紀 *Ben Ji,* or "Basic Annals," complete in twenty-five chapters and seven volumes, take precedence as of right. These "Basic Annals" are essentially a chronicle of the court and of important affairs in the empire as a whole which are directed from the capital. In this connection it should be remembered that the provincial authorities enjoyed under the empire a very considerable measure of local autonomy and responsibility. The sequence of entries is rather rigidly fixed by precedent in order of importance: imperial ritual observances; calamities, signs, and portents; personal acts of the emperor; conferments, appointments, transfers, and dismissals; government business; movements of imperial troops; remissions of taxation for relief of distress; population and revenue; and presentation of tribute.

The second section of the history comprises a series of sixteen 志 *Jir,* "Essays," each devoted to some special topic which is treated as a whole from beginning to end of the dynasty. This section fills 37 volumes which are divided into 142 chapters. The subjects treated afford a broad view of the concerns of Chinese government, and their sequence suggests the relative importance which is assigned to them by tradition:

---

[23] Erich Haenisch, "Das Ts'ing-shi-kao und die sonstige chinesische Literatur zur Geschichte der letzten 300 Jahre," *Asia Major,* VI, no. 4 (Leipzig, 1930), 403–444. Withdrawn in 1928, it was again released for sale at the beginning of 1937.

astronomy, calamities and prodigies, the calendar,
geography, ritual, music, sumptuary regulations, selection of officials by examination, government offices,
economics, waterways, war, justice, literature, com-
munications, and foreign relations.

The third division is composed of 表 *Biao*, "Tables,"
in 53 chapters and 30 volumes. These set forth the
genealogy of the sons and daughters of emperors, of
the more distant imperial relatives, and of officials who
received titles of hereditary nobility. Later tables
record the succession of Grand Secretaries, Ministers
of the Military Council, and the chief officers of the
central and provincial administrations. The last tables
contain genealogies of the Mongolian princes and the
chronology of the exchange of foreign envoys.

The fourth and last portion, comprising 316 chapters
in 57 volumes, or nearly half the work, is devoted to
列傳 *Lieh Juan*, "Biographies." These, classified primarily according to the character of their subjects, and
secondarily on a chronological basis, include all the
chief personages of the entire period, including many
who, because they did not live in close contact with
the court or with the government, are accorded no
mention in the "Basic Annals."

It will at once be seen that the several portions of
this composite work, as is the case with every standard
history, are intended to be mutually complementary
and are necessary to each other if a well rounded view
of the past is desired. Any single portion is to be regarded, from the Western point of view, rather as material for history than as history itself.

It has been observed that the traditional Chinese

scheme of classification divides "history" into fifteen categories, among which the standard histories hold first place. The formal pattern received what may be considered its final and most detailed crystallization in the "Complete Work of the Four Treasuries"[24] which was compiled under imperial direction, for the most part during the decade 1772–1781. Concise tabulation may suffice to reveal the dominant characteristics of this pattern.

1. 正史 *Jeng Shir*, "Standard Histories." These are distinguished by form, by the sources from which they are drawn and by official recognition.

2. 編年 *Bien Nien*, "Annals." This classification is based solely on form, which is very nearly that of the chronicles which constitute the backbone of the standard histories, except that no restrictions are imposed regarding the length or scope of the compilation. Arrangement of whatever material is selected for presentation must be strictly chronological.

3. 紀事本末 *Ji Shir Ben Mo*, "Narratives from Beginning to End." Each of the works referred to this category treats completely a single subject or period. It may be viewed as a whole, without restriction to close chronological sequence, or may be divided into sections each of which is treated independently. The form of composition, either of the whole or of the parts, may be precisely that of the Annals.

4. 別史 *Bieh Shir*, "Separate Histories." This extensive group embraces most of the more considerable histories which do not conform exactly to any of the preceding three pre-

---

[24] The 四庫全書 *Sz ku tsüan shu*, which embraces 3,462 works in 36,300 volumes, proved too big to print (cf. *supra*, chap. III, n. 48 and n. 60); but the classification scheme adopted for it is known through extremely influential catalogues. Cf. *infra*, n. 28.

scriptions. It is distinctly a "leftover" category, to which, however, many important works belong.[25]

5. 雜史 *Dza Shir*, "Miscellaneous Histories." No definite rule appears to distinguish this group from the preceding one. In general, works of small scope or compass are relegated to this division.

6. 詔令奏議 *Jao Ling Dzou I*, "Decrees, Mandates, Memorials, and Recommendations." This category includes various extensive repertories of state papers published by imperial authority, and also many more modest collections of the advice tendered to the throne by individual statesmen. Decrees and mandates emanate of course from the sovereign or in times of weakness are issued in his name. Memorials are written representations to the emperor on the initiative of a subject; recommendations are made in response to imperial demand.

7. 傳記 *Juan Ji*, "Biographical Memoirs." This category is closely associated with the foregoing by the fact that the Chinese idea of the biography of a statesman is hardly more than a record of his more significant state papers: the private life of subjects as of emperors is rarely touched upon. The great number of works embraced in this group may be guessed from the predominant part in the standard histories occupied by biography. Closely linked to them, too, although they are accorded a separate major classification as one of the "four treasuries," are the editions of "individual authors," many of which are particularly important for biography, not merely as raw source material (the writings of the individuals concerned), but because they frequently contain 年譜 *nien pu* or "chronological biographies." These last are in fact often the only source from which can be extracted the dates of birth and death, usually ignored by the Chinese in favor of the date of the doctoral examination.

[25] Included in it are two works which conform strictly to the "standard history" specifications: the 明史稿 *Ming shir gao*, "Draft Ming History" of 王鴻緒 Wang Hung-sü, 315 chapters, 80 volumes, and the "Draft Tsing History."

8. 史鈔 *Shir Chao,* "Historical Excerpts." This fortunately limited class consists in verbal transcriptions, chiefly from the standard histories, without — in theory — any modification of the text.

9. 載記 *Tsai Ji,* "Contemporaneous Records." A small group of works devoted to the history of those concurrent smaller Chinese states which are regarded as illegitimate, and to the history and description of neighboring countries.

10. 時令 *Shir Ling,* "Regulation of Time" or "Chronography." Inasmuch as dynastic prosperity has always been considered by the Chinese to be closely bound up with the orderliness of seasonal change, works on the measurement and division of time have been accorded by them an importance quite foreign to our thought.

11. 地理 *Di Li,* "Geography." This is considerably the largest division of the historical treasury. Within it, in addition to treatises on historical geography, fall thousands of works which have been variously called gazetteers or local histories. These works ordinarily seek to give, for a specific area, its topography, administrative history with tables of past officials, its economic status, biographies of distinguished native sons of all periods, account of its temples and antiquities, its history and local traditions, and its literature. There exists at least one such work for every province, prefecture, and sub-prefecture of the empire, and for almost every district, or even village of importance.[26]

12. 職官 *Jir Guan,* "Functions and Offices." A small group of special treatises on the evolution of ófficial designations and functions.

13. 政書 *Jeng Shu,* "Treatises on Government." An important series of compilations which set forth comprehensively and in detail the whole complicated fabric of governmental machinery under successive dynasties. In this category are usually placed certain large works which differ from ency-

[26] Pelliot, BEFEO, VIII (1908), 519–520; A. W. Hummel, *Report of the Librarian of Congress, Division of Orientalia, 1931–32* (Washington, 1933), 193–194. Cf. *supra,* chap. II, n. 17.

clopedias only slightly in form [27] but of which the subject matter is approximately the same as that of the "Essays" in the "Standard Histories," problems of governmental concern.

14. 目錄 *Mu Lu*, "Catalogues." This division embraces not only bibliography, but also repertories of epigraphy. Chinese scholars have very seldom until quite recent times attempted to provide any bibliographic guidance to readers. The "General Catalogue of the 'Complete Work of the Four Treasuries,'" [28] which was published in 1789, and the abridged version of it, which was issued seven years earlier, were unprecedented not merely in size, but in the regular inclusion of extended critical comment upon the substance of the books recorded. Previous (and most later) bibliographic labors were devoted rather to inventory of titles in a library or of rare editions known to a bibliophile. The first serious effort to furnish elementary guidance for the student is the "Answers to Queries on Bibliography" [29] by 繆荃孫 Miao Tsüan-sun, which was published in 1875 at the instance of 張之洞 Jang Jir-dung, a statesman with numerous foreign contacts.

15. 史評 *Shir Ping*, "Historical Criticism." Precisely because personal comment in historical composition is sharply restricted by tradition, historians have sometimes gathered their critical observations upon the works of others,[30]

---

[27] Cf. Pelliot's review of Courant's *Catalogue*, BEFEO, I, 146.

[28] 四庫全書總目 *Sz Ku Tsüan Shu dzung mu*, 200 chapters, 92 volumes (palace edition). Critical notices are extended beyond the 3,462 works accepted for the select library to 6,734 others of lesser merit.

[29] 書目答問 *Shu mu da wen*, 1 large volume. Cf. *supra*, chap. III, n. 13.

[30] A cardinal place in the still unwritten history of this branch of Chinese historiography will be reserved to the 史通 *Shir tung*, "Historical Perspectives," of 劉知幾 Liu Jir-ji (661–721), 20 chapters, 4 volumes (四部叢刊 *Sz bu tsung kan* edition). It circulates commonly in modern editions with comment compiled by a Tsing scholar, 浦起龍 Pu Chi-lung: 史通通釋 *Shir tung tung shir*, 10 volumes.

or even upon their own,[31] into special compilations which are entirely devoted to them, just as in early ages commentary was transmitted separately from the classic texts.[32] The category is a small one.

It will have been observed that among these fifteen departments of "history," the first five are distinguished one from another by largely superficial criteria. In order to gain full knowledge of the mere chronological sequence of events, we must consult in turn the standard history, annals, complete narratives, independent and miscellaneous histories of a given period.[33]

[31] An important precedent was established by 司馬光 Sz-ma Guang (1019–1086) who published the 資治通鑑考異 Dz Jir Tung Jien kao i, "Examination of Divergencies from the 'Complete Mirror for Aid in Government,'" 30 chapters, 6 volumes (Sz bu tsung kan edition), as a commentary on his own great work. Cf. supra, chap. II, n. 12.

[32] Cf. supra, p. 20.

[33] This may be well illustrated by reference to some of the more important sources for Sung history. The standard 宋史 Sung shir, 496 chapters, 100 volumes (1739 palace edition), of course opens with the "Basic Annals" of the dynasty, which occupy chapters 1–47 or 10 volumes. The 建炎以來繫年要錄 Jien Yen i lai ji nien yao lu, or "Record of Important Events Since the Jien Yen Era," 200 chapters, 64 volumes, is wholly devoted to the detailed annals of the reign of Emperor 高宗 Gao Dzung, 1127–1162. Closely linked with it is the 三朝北盟會編 San chao bei meng hui bien, "Compendium on the Northern Alliance under Three Reigns," which recounts in 40 volumes the whole history of Sung relations with the 金 Jin Tartars, 1117–1161, including the reign of Gao Dzung. Yet this work, of which 245 out of 250 chapters are compiled in pure "annal" form, is classed as a "narrative from beginning to end" simply because it treats completely the subject delimited by the title. With these works, again, should surely be placed the 四朝別史 Sz chao bieh shir, "Separate Histories of Four Dynasties," a group of five smaller works which, as the name implies, have been classed among the "separate histories." One, the 東都事略 Dung Du shir lüeh or "Résumé of Affairs at the Eastern

We in the West are accustomed to single out from among our sources those which bear direct independent witness to the march of events or to the circumstances which surround and condition them. We then proclaim, "These are our primary sources; the rest are but secondary." Such procedure is, however, practicable in China to only a very limited extent, because of the method of compilation employed by Chinese historians.[34] The category of documents may, indeed, well be respected as a fairly homogeneous group of primary materials. But so many contemporary records have been verbally imbedded at least in part in later compilations of various categories, that it may almost be said of Chinese history that it consists exclusively of primary sources. Glaring and lamentable as are the defects in the traditional technique of Chinese historians, their work has drawn from the very primitiveness of their synthetic method, coupled with an age-long insistence on intellectual integrity, a kind of rugged strength and fundamental reliability which constitute valid claims upon our respect and admiration. No other ancient nation possesses records of its whole past so voluminous, so continuous, or so accurate.

Capital" (汴梁 Bien Liang, modern Kaifeng), deals with the history of the Northern Sung (960–1126); another, the 南宋書 *Nan Sung shu*, the "History of the Southern Sung" (1127–1279); while the others are devoted to the various Tartar invaders, Liao, Jin, and Yüan, who drove the Sung first across the Long River and finally from their throne. A whole series of lesser compilations now listed as "miscellaneous histories," deal with precisely the same epoch. Cf., e.g., the 國學圖書館圖書總目 *Guo Hsüeh Tu-shu-guan tu shu dzung mu*, "General Catalogue of the Sinological Library" (Nanking), X, 14b.

[34] Cf. *supra*, pp. 70–71.

ADDITIONS AND CORRECTIONS

(Prepared with the assistance of Yang Lien-sheng)

Page 3, line 2, add note: For attempts made by Chinese and Japanese scholars to write such a history, cf. 金毓黻 Jin Yü-fu, 中國史學史 *Jung-guo shir-shüeh shir*, "A History of Chinese Historiography" (1944), and 內藤虎次郎 Naitō Torajirō, 支那史學史 *Shina shigaku shi*, "A History of Chinese Historiography" (1949), the latter being a posthumous publication.

Page 5, line 31, add: Three more volumes of the *Gu shir bien* have been published, vol. 5 (1935) edited by Gu Jieh-gang, vol. 6 (1938) by Lo Gen-dze, and vol. 7 (1941) in three parts by 楊寬 Yang Kuan.

Page 7, line 26: for 9e *read* 10e

Page 9, line 2: for sheep bones *read* cattle bones

——, *line 21, add:* Also cf. Karlgren, "Glosses on the Book of Documents," *BMFEA* 20 (1948), 21 (1949).

Page 11, lines 15–16: for his highest official title, 孔夫子 Kung Fu-dz, "the Hon. Kung" *read* the intimate but respectful name, 孔夫子 Kung Fu-dz, "Master Kung."

Page 12, line 31, add: Also cf. Chi Sz-ho, "Professor Hung on the Ch'un-ch'iu," *Yenching Journal of Social Studies* 1 (1938) 48–71, and 春秋經傳引得 *Chun-chiu jing-juan yin-de*, Harvard-Yenching Institute Sinological Index Series, Supplement 11 (1937).

Page 14, line 14: for Abridged View *read* Outlines and Details

Page 16, line 33, add: Also cf. Burton Watson, *Ssu-Ma Ch'ien, Grand Historian of China* (1958).

Page 21, line 29, add: Also cf. Hu Shir, "A Note on Ch'üan Tsu-wang, Chao I-ch'ing and Tai Chen," in

107

Eminent Chinese of the Ch'ing Period (1644–1912), ed. by Arthur W. Hummel (1944), pp. 970–982.

Page 24, line 22, add: Also cf. 張心澂 Jang Shin-cheng, 偽書通考 *Wei-shu tung-kao*, "A Comprehensive Investigation of Forgeries in Books" (1939), in two volumes.

Page 39, line 27: for pp. 47–69. *read* pp. 47–69, revised by L. Carrington Goodrich (1955).

Page 44, line 29: for 247–258. *read* 247–258, also translated by 鄭德坤 Jeng De-kun, "The Travels of Emperor Mu," *JNChBRAS* 64 (1933) 124–142, 65 (1934) 128–149.

Page 45, line 38, add: Also cf. Lionel Giles, *Six Centuries at Tunhuang* (1944), and his *Descriptive Catalogue of the Chinese Manuscripts from Tunhuang in the British Museum* (1957).

Page 55, line 19, add: Also cf. J. R. Hightower, *Han shih wai chuan, Han Ying's Illustrations of the Didactic Application of the Classic of Songs* (1952).

Page 55, line 39, add: For a very scholarly translation and textual criticism of the *Shir jing*, cf. Karlgren, "Glosses on the Kuo feng Odes," *BMFEA* 14 (1942), "Glosses on the Siao ya Odes" and "The Book of Odes, Kuo feng and Siao ya," *BMFEA* (1944), "The Book of Odes, Ta ya and Sung," *BMFEA* 17 (1945), and "Glosses on the Ta ya and Sung Odes," *BMFEA* 18 (1946), or Karlgren, *The Book of Odes* (1950).

Page 60, line 22, add: Also cf. *The Analects of Confucius*, translated and annotated by Arthur Waley (1938).

Page 67, line 33, add: The term *gu shir*, however, is also used to mean "precedents," and books bearing the title *gu shir* in this sense often contain important information on institutions of a dynasty.

Page 74, line 31: for *Sz lin dzi lüeh* read *Tsz lin dzi lüeh*

Page 81, line 33, add: Also cf. Homer H. Dubs, "Chinese Imperial Designations," *JAOS* 65 (1945) 26–33.

Page 82, line 10: for 燁 *read* 號.

Page 87, line 32, add: Also cf. Homer H. Dubs, *History of the Former Han Dynasty*, 1 (1938), 2 (1944), 3 (1955).

Page 88, line 9, add note: For more information on the Standard Histories, cf. Yang Lien-sheng, *Topics in Chinese History* (1950), pp. 32–38 (notes prepared by Professor L. C. Goodrich). Also cf. Yang Lien-sheng, "The Organization of Chinese Official Historiography," to appear in *Historians of China and Japan*, edited by W. G. Beasley and E. G. Pulleyblank, to be published by the Oxford University Press. A German version of this article, "Die Organisation der chinesischen offiziellen Geschichtsschreibung," has been published in *Saeculum* 8 (1957) 196–209. A very useful reference work is Hans H. Frankel, *Catalogue of Translations from the Chinese Dynastic Histories for the Period 220–960* (1957).

Pages 90–91, note 10, omit the first three sentences. Here 諸 = 之於.

Page 91, line 6, add note: For an example of early *shir lu*, cf. Bernard S. Solomon, *The Veritable Record of the T'ang Emperor Shun-tsung* (1955).

Page 93, line 18: for 歲 *read* 戌.

Page 95, line 35, add: Also cf. J. K. Fairbank and Deng Sz-yü, "On the Types and Uses of Ch'ing Documents," *HJAS* 5 (1940) 1–71 or their *Ch'ing Administration: Three Studies* (1960).

Page 103, line 4, add note: The category *jeng-shu*

includes important encyclopedias dealing with government such as the 通典 *Tung dien* by 杜佑 Du Yu (735–812), the 文獻通考 *Wen-shien tung-kao* by 馬端臨 Ma Duan-lin (13th century), and the various 會要 *hui-yao;* cf. Deng Sz-yü and Knight Biggerstaff, *An Annotated Bibliography of Selected Chinese Reference Works* (rev. ed., 1950), pp. 146–164.

———, *line 38, add:* Professor William Hung has been preparing a monograph on Liu Jir-ji and his *Shir-tung;* also cf. 高柄翊 Byongik Koh, "Zur Werttheorie in der chinesischen Historiographie auf Grund des Shin-t'ung des Liu Chih-chi (661–721)," 震檀學報 *The Chintan Hakpo* 18 (1957) 87–130, 19 (1958) 81–163. On another important author in Chinese historiography, 章學誠 Jang Shüeh-cheng (1738–1801) and his 文史通義 *Wen shir tung-i,* David S. Nivison has a monograph which will be published by the Stanford University Press.

Page 104, line 23: for *Jien Yen i lai ji* read *Jien Yen i lai shi*

INDEX

INDEX

Accuracy, criteria of, 66–67
Alteration of texts, 47–52, 54, 61
Anachronism, 25–29
"Analects of Confucius," 59 n.74; 61 n.80.
"Ancient Texts," xv; 19 n.4; 22–29nn.; 32 n.32; 40 n.50; 79 n.1
Annals (class), 100
"Annals Written on Bamboo," cf. *Ju shu ji nien*
Archaeology, 44–46
Archaic text, 8 n.2; 56–62
Archival Division of the Palace Museum, 91 n.10; 94 n.17; 95 n.18
Archival records (feudal), 10–12
Archives of the Grand Secretariat, 90 n.10; 93–95nn.
Aurousseau, Léonard, 39–40nn.; 46 n.57; 84 n.11; 91 n.12
Authentication
  through repugnant criticism, 29–30
  through independent citations, 30–31
  through bibliographic record, 32–44
"Authenticity of Ancient Chinese Texts, The"; cf. "Ancient Texts"
Authorship, 23–24
"Autour d'une traduction sanscrite du Tao To King," 29 n.26

Background, omission of, 76
Ban Biao, 9 n.3
Ban Gu, 20 n.7; 26 n.18; 32–37, 53
Ban Gu nien pu, 32 n.34
Barnes, H. E., 5 n.4
"Basic Annals," cf. *Ben ji*
Bei Lin, 61 n.80
"Beiträge zur Mandjurischen Bibliographie und Literatur," 92 n.15
ben (volume), 41

Ben ji ("Basic annals"), 71, 74, 76, 88, 94, 98
Bi Ren Tang, 62 n.80
Bi Sung Lou tsang shu jir, 24 n.13; 40 n.49
bi yung (insular academy), 34 n.37
Biao ("Tables"), 99
"Bibliography of the Chinese Imperial Collections of Literature," 48 n.60
"Bibliothèque médiévale retrouvée au Kan-sou, Une," 20 n.7; 46 n.56
Bieh lu, 37 n.40
Bieh shir (class), 100
Bien nien (class), 100
Biggerstaff, Knight, 92 n.15; 96 n.20
Biographical Memoirs (class), 101
"Biographies," 99
"Biographies of Great and Meritorious Ministers of the Reigning Dynasty," 96 n.20
Biot, Edouard, 8 n.1; 18 n.2; 32 n.33; 56 n.69
Blake, R. P., ix
Block printing, 39, 47–49
Bruce, J. P., 14 n.11
Bureau of National Historiography, 91 n.10; 96
Bureau of Tsing History, 94 n.17; 95 n.18

Cabinet Library, 39 n.48
Calendars, diverse, 71
Cameron, M. E., 26 n.19
"Canon of Change," 57, 59; 61 n.80
"Canon of Filial Piety," 61 n.80
"Canon of History," cf. *Shu jing*
Carter, T. F., 39 n.47; 50 n.61
Catalogues (class), 103
Causation, 77
Censorship, 14 n.13
Chambeau, 73 n.9

113

Harvard Historical Monographs

*Out of print

1. Athenian Tribal Cycles in the Hellenistic Age. By W. S. Ferguson. 1932.
2. The Private Record of an Indian Governor-Generalship. The Correspondence of Sir John Shore, Governor-General, with Henry Dundas, President of the Board of Control, 1793–1798. Edited by Holden Furber. 1933.
3. The Federal Railway Land Subsidy Policy of Canada. By J. B. Hedges. 1934.
4. Russian Diplomacy and the Opening of the Eastern Question in 1838 and 1839. By P. E. Mosely. 1934.
5. The First Social Experiments in America. A Study in the Development of Spanish Indian Policy in the Sixteenth Century. By Lewis Hanke. 1935.*
6. British Propaganda at Home and in the United States from 1914 to 1917. By J. D. Squires. 1935.*
7. Bernadotte and the Fall of Napoleon. By F. D. Scott. 1935.
8. The Incidence of the Terror during the French Revolution. A Statistical Interpretation. By Donald Greer. 1935.*
9. French Revolutionary Legislation on Illegitimacy, 1789–1804. By Crane Brinton. 1936.*
10. An Ecclesiastical Barony of the Middle Ages. The Bishopric of Bayeaux, 1066–1204. By S. E. Gleason. 1936.
11. Chinese Traditional Historiography. By C. S. Gardner. 1938.
12. Studies in Early French Taxation. By J. R. Strayer and C. H. Taylor. 1939.
13. Muster and Review. A Problem of English Military Administration 1420–1440. By R. A. Newhall. 1940.
14. Portuguese Voyages to America in the Fifteenth Century. By S. E. Morison. 1940.*

36. Historical Pessimism in the French Enlightenment. By Henry Vyverberg. 1958.
37. The Renaissance Idea of Wisdom. By Eugene F. Rice, Jr. 1958
38. The First Professional Revolutionist: Filippo Michele Buonarroti (1761–1837). By Elizabeth L. Eisenstein. 1959.
39. The Formation of the Baltic States: A Study of the Effects of Great Power Politics upon the Emergence of Lithuania, Latvia, and Estonia. By Stanley W. Page. 1959.
40. Conservation and the Gospel of Efficiency: The Progressive Conservation Movement, 1890-1920. By Samuel P. Hays. 1959.
41. The Urban Frontier: The Rise of Western Cities, 1790-1830. By Richard C. Wade. 1959.
42. New Zealand, 1769–1840: Early Years of Western Contact. By Harrison M. Wright. 1959.
43. Ottoman Imperialism and German Protestantism, 1521–1555. By Stephen A. Fischer-Galati. 1959.
44. Foch versus Clemenceau: France and German Dismemberment, 1918–1919. By Jere Clemens King. 1960.
45. Steelworkers in America: The Nonunion Era. By David Brody. 1960.
46. Carroll Wright and Labor Reform: The Origin of Labor Statistics. By James Leiby. 1960.
47. Chōshū in the Meiji Restoration. By Albert M. Craig. 1961.